With prose as living and ~~~
burrows deep into the themes of Lent to reveal what was lost
in Eden, and what can be found beginning in Gethsemane.
Finding Life is a profound yet practical Lenten companion
with lessons to nourish our faith and enrich our spirit.

—LYNN AUSTIN, speaker, author of nineteen books,
including *Historical Christian Fiction*

Making Lent real—in season or out—takes courage. When I'd
rather stay sleeping outside the garden with the disciples, Jane
gently, with real-life stories and engaging insight from the
Bible, leads me from Eden's story into Gethsemane's to make
our Lord's story real in my life. What a brilliant connection
between the two gardens! Let Jane lead you there—where the
cross comes alive and Easter morning resounds with joy.

—THADDEUS BARNUM, author *Real Identity*, senior pastor,
Church of the Apostles, Fairfield, Connecticut

Jane Rubietta's devotionals are a lovely, deep-soaking rain to
my parched soul. Her writing disciples me, and yet its beauty
also leaves me feeling as if I've lingered in a garden just for
the sake of enjoying it. I will definitely return to this place she
has so artfully cultivated again and again.

—DIANNE E. BUTTS, author of six books including
Prophecies Fulfilled in the Birth of Jesus and *Deliver Me*

Jane turns our hearts toward the beauty God blossoms into our
lives through Lent, or for any time of the year that we would
seek Him. Let her words move you into the garden of God's
wisdom, love, and care. There she will show you how to spend
time reflecting, pondering, and enjoying the Creator, realizing
His plan from before Eden to beyond Gethsemane

—PAM FARREL, author of nearly forty books including
Becoming a Brave New Woman, *Woman of Influence*,
and *Men are Like Waffles, Women are Like Spaghetti*

What a beautiful invitation to transformation! Jane takes you by the hand and gently leads you on a journey from Eden to Gethsemane. Each step of the journey leads you closer to the heart of Jesus. There, in His holy presence, you find what you are most longing for—intimacy with Christ and newness of life!

—BECKY HARLING, speaker, author of *The 30 Day Praise Challenge*

Jane Rubietta brings a sensitivity to her writing that establishes an immediate bond between Jane and her readers. Whether her setting is a church potluck or a profound passage of Scripture, her insights are wise, her lessons are practical, and her message is encouraging. Read and be refreshed!

—DR. DENNIS E. HENSLEY, author of *Jesus in the 9 to 5*

In her book *Finding Life*, Jane Rubietta issues a delightful invitation "to come to the garden and walk with Jesus." With the tone and touch of an attentive gardener, she leads the reader down a path of rich and varied discovery . . . of life. Take the walk with her from Eden to Gethsemane and find life.

—BOB HOSTETLER, author of *Life Stinks . . . and Then You Die (Living Well in a Sick World)*

A question at the heart of this book penetrated my own heart: "How much of this hunger for beauty is rooted in Eden, our longing for an idyllic place of existence? In an ache to find our life, in the very deepest sense?" So much of what plagues our lives is simply because we cannot find that perfect place of peace. In *Finding Life*, Jane Rubietta has answered this question simply beautifully.

—LANE P. JORDAN, author, international speaker, singer, life coach

Jane's authentic writing glimpses life's sojourn in ways that cultivate heartfelt introspection and a deeper kind of devotion. Caringly, she unearths the roots that connect us to the gardens of Eden and Gethsemane, in the process revealing God's transformational garden-work for our souls.

—BISHOP JONATHON KEATON, United Methodist Church

Jane Rubietta's writing is so powerful, visual, and impactful—she is a gifted wordsmith who captures the essence of developing an intimate connection with God, while challenging the reader to do the same. *Finding Life* is filled with practical applications and opportunities for personal reflection. Don't miss it!

—CAROL KENT, speaker, best-selling author of
When I Lay My Isaac Down and *Unquenchable*

These are transformational devotionals with depth. Jane offers a fresh and compelling vision of both gardens—Eden and Gethsemane. But more than pluming depths, she has coupled biblical truth with practical ways in which to personally restore what has been destroyed. Especially transformational can be her guide, which leads one to read, contemplate, and act. There is rich and practical depth in these pages.

—JO ANNE LYON, General Superintendent, The Wesleyan Church

Finding Life by Jane Rubietta is a lovely story of life given, lost, and gloriously found, all within the context of two great gardens. This is a devotional that also is a study in discipleship, yet which carries readers along through its exquisitely told journey. More than a deeply personal Bible study in devotion, this is also a perfect discipleship tool for small groups.

—KATHI MACIAS, award-winning author of more than
forty books, including *The Singing Quilt*

In *Finding Life*, Jane Rubietta offers an honest and grace-filled guide to faith by bringing readers on a journey through the gardens of Scripture, from creation to crucifixion and beyond. Through exquisitely rich stories and images, Jane gently encourages readers to connect with Jesus, learn from revered spiritual teachers, and examine their own faith lives. *Finding Life* will be a blessing to both individuals and groups.

—ROCHELLE MELANDER, certified professional coach, author of
A Generous Presence: Spiritual Leadership and the Art of Coaching

My search for a Lenten devotional guide to address the weariness of my soul has ended. Jane Rubietta provides this in her book *Finding Life*. She chooses themes like coping with fractured relationships and shame, dealing with failure and suffering. Never offering simplistic solutions, Jane traces these universal realities from the garden of Eden, through the truths of Scripture into the garden of Gethsemane, finding there the life offered today by the resurrected Christ. The journey is an honest and sometimes challenging one. But in these pages is a place where the Holy Spirit communes with our spirit and leads us gently to the light. This book will be treasured by those who desire to deepen their faith during Lent or at any other time of the year.

—ELEANOR SHEPHERD, author of award-winning
More Questions than Answers: Sharing Faith by Listening

Jane Rubietta's *Finding Life* takes us through the baggage of life—darkness, shame, work, failure, and more—and points us to the garden of God's presence. Each of the forty in-depth reflections concludes with a penetrating "So what?"question, which makes this book so useful. It made me stop and look at myself. More importantly, it pointed me to the garden of a better place in life. I will give copies to friends.

—GLEN SHEPHERD, president and CEO,
Health Partners International of Canada

In these pages is delightful garden of rich inspiration springing out of Jane Rubietta's artful words of devotion. Passing through the darkness from Eden, she leads us through the promise of Gethsemane, which will spring full bloom into your soul.

—LINDA EVANS SHEPHERD, author of *Experiencing God's Presence: Learning to Listen While You Pray*

Jane Rubietta invites us on a journey from Eden to Gethsemane that will surprise and inspire you. Packed with Scripture and written with personal witness and wisdom, this forty-day adventure calls us to not only understand but also live into the promise of full, new life.

—REV. ANDREA SUMMERS, director of ministry for women, The Wesleyan Church

As "deep calls to deep," this book touches the heart of the soul. Jane Rubietta takes us on a reflective, spiritual journey from Eden through Gethsemane to the garden tomb with powerful insights all along the way. This is more than a casual read. It is a heartfelt experience.

—MARK O. WILSON, pastor, author of *Filled Up, Poured Out: How God's Spirit Can Revive Your Passion and Purpose*

FINDING LIFE

FROM EDEN TO GETHSEMANE— THE GARDEN RESTORED

Jane Rubietta

wphonline.com

Copyright © 2014 by Jane Rubietta
Published by Wesleyan Publishing House
Indianapolis, Indiana 46250
Printed in the United States of America
ISBN: 978-0-89827-892-7
ISBN (e-book): 978-0-89827-893-4

Library of Congress Cataloging-in-Publication Data

Rubietta, Jane.
  [Between two gardens]
  Finding life : from Eden to Gethsemane, the garden restored / Jane Rubietta.
     pages cm
  Originally published under title: Between two gardens : from Eden to Gethsemane :
Minneapolis, Minn. : Bethany House, c2001.
  Includes bibliographical references.
  ISBN 978-0-89827-892-7
1. Gardeners--Prayers and devotions. 2. Gardens--Religious aspects--Christianity--
Meditations. I. Title.
  BV4596.G36R83 2014
  242--dc23
                              2013039148

This book was previously published as *Between Two Gardens* by Bethany House, 2001.

Finding Life is dedicated to two women whose lives and prayers introduced me to the Gardener. They live with Him now, and I laugh to imagine all their gardening questions when they walk and talk with Jesus. Mary Ruth "Cookie" Parker, and my great aunt, Mae Tucker—your love for God and for blooming things made the world, and my heart, a more beautiful place.

CONTENTS

ACKNOWLEDGEMENTS

"Thank you" only begins to express the role these people have played in my life and spiritual development. Even so, inadequate as it is, huge thanks to these special people.

To my garden friends in Joliet, Illinois, who tutored me in gardening: Len Hooper, Debbie Huckstep, Jackie Garton, and Kathy Fairbairn. Before that, Gayle Huebner and her magical touch with flowers impacted me profoundly.

To dear friends Ellen Binder and Kay Frahm, who, trowels and all, loaded precious keepsakes and plants and blooming bulbs into the car and trekked through eighteen inches of snow to help me create our first meditative garden at a women's retreat. From that retreat grew the essence of this book. I thank God for you both!

To Sandra Fricke and her family, whose love of gardens was reflected in her careful tending of the yard that would one day become a setting in which to write this book.

To my grandparents: Bill and Betty Houpt and Jack and Jeppie Henderson, whose luxurious plantings, whether tomatoes or roses or cotton or crocuses, form my earliest memories. Thank you for your passion for the land and for beauty.

Other special friends have kept me sowing and reaping:

Lin Johnson (Word-Pro Communications and the Write-to-Publish Conference): You are officially my mentor and friend for life. The entire trajectory of my life changed when I walked into your writers' conference for the first time.

My covenant group, who for years modeled Christ-like living to me: Adele Calhoun, Karen Mains, Linda Richardson, Marilyn Stewart, and Sibyl Towner.

My amazing writers' group, Lynn Austin and Cleo Lampos. What would I do without you? Probably eat fewer brownies. But such a harvest of words since we've been together.

I could not write a word without the loving support and noise level and humor of my family. Thank you for tolerating poor meals, empty refrigerators, and forgetfulness. Your growth challenges me to live out of the fullness of Christ's work in Gethsemane. Thank you, Rich, Ruthie, Zak, and Josh. And now, Matt and baby Abby. I love you. May you know, deep in the soil of your soul, the depth of God's love for you.

INTRODUCTION

Because nature speaks to my soul in a profound, nonverbal language, I've tried to create gardens in every location that my family has lived. Gardens bear witness to God's world of incredible creativity—of God's love displayed for all of us through creation.

How much of this hunger for beauty is rooted in Eden, our longing for an idyllic place of existence? In an ache to find our life, in the very deepest sense? Every generation, it seems, seeks for Eden in some form or another. Various searches for paradise, for utopia, for the ideal society, for the fountain of youth and the Holy Grail have occupied and obsessed people through the ages.

Daily catalogs, fliers, and ads filled with gorgeous flowers and promising award-winning gardens land in my mailbox and inbox. Cars jam the parking lots as people stream into stores for the perfect seed, plant, trowel, and growth-producing compound. Weekend gardeners sweat over the curse of Adam (weeds) and mow down the grass that's sprouted from their fertilizing efforts. Birdbaths, rock gardens, and fishponds guarantee retailers a better bottom line and tempt buyers with a piece of the peace of Eden. Resort and vacation packages lure travelers with lush garden settings and the hope of genuine and permanent restoration.

One summer, frustration drew me more deeply into the Scriptures. Looking out over our sun-parched grass, my soul thirsted for the watering of God. Even as record-breaking heat scorched the Midwest, my soul withered right alongside the garden plants. Verses such as Jeremiah 31:12 sowed desire in my heart, longing and disbelief springing up together: "Their soul shall be as a watered garden" (KJV).

Jesus' uses of gardening terms and themes whispered hope to me. "I am the vine, you are the branches" (John 15:5); "faith the size of a mustard seed" (Matt. 17:20); "the sower went out to sow" (Matt. 13:3). Jesus' listeners understood agriculture, farming, and hoeing out a living. Certainly Jesus spoke the language of His culture, a culture based on the fruit of the land. But, just as surely, His language points out a deeper importance. Because the exile that began in the garden of Eden ends in another garden, the garden of Gethsemane.

PARALLEL GARDENS

Surprising parallels between Eden and Gethsemane challenge us to make this journey, to traverse the distance.

They beckon us into a new, full, blooming place. They murmur that on this sojourn, we will find our life. In between these gardens, we land in another plot of land, a place where I wonder if God intended to conclude the exile when leading the Israelites to the Promised Land. At the very least, Israel is a type of Eden, a place where the God who walked about Eden would tend the land: "For the land, into which you are entering to possess it, is not like the land of Egypt from which you came, where you used to sow your seed and water it with your foot like a vegetable garden. But the land into which you are about to cross to possess it, a land of hills and valleys, drinks water from the rain of heaven, a land for which the LORD your God cares; the eyes of the LORD your God are always on it, from the beginning even to the end of the year" (Deut. 11:10–12).

But no. The Israelites' refusal to enter this next garden, this place of promise, leads us into the life of Jesus, nudging us nearer to that final garden.

As we edge closer to the garden of Gethsemane, we find Jesus returning there again and again. The Scriptures say, "He came out and proceeded as was His custom to the Mount of Olives; and the disciples also followed Him" (Luke 22:39). His custom? Yes. Jesus frequented this place, this garden. Luke 21:37 says He taught during the day in the temple and at evening headed out to "spend the night on the mount that is called Olivet."

Jesus met with His disciples in a garden, prayed in a garden, was violently arrested in a garden, and was buried in a garden tomb.

In the garden, He would wrestle again with the serpent of temptation; Christ would rely once again on the power of God to sustain Him. In the garden, He would pray with such agony that an angel would appear from heaven, strengthening Him (Luke 22:43).

Uncomfortably, we land somewhere between two gardens, between Eden and Gethsemane. Though Christ completed His work in the garden of Gethsemane, we so rarely stand in that completion. We strive for the final garden but are often mired in the mud and matted with the dust left over from Eden's exile. While we still experience some of the curses of fleeing, while we seek continually the fruit of the Promised Land, we remain, somehow, outside the gates of that garden.

We don't live in the full completion of Christ's work in Gethsemane. Suffering exists in this world; thorns prick; the shame initiated when Adam and Eve's eyes were opened still paralyzes. Fear of intimacy roots us to the ground, keeping us from bonding to others and to God. We don't always hear the voice that Adam and Eve heard in the cool of the garden; nor do we recognize Christ's voice speaking to us. And so it goes. Fellowship is hindered, we cannot see God face-to-face, pain continues, and the serpent still tempts and throws dice for our soul.

And yet, Christ could say, "It is finished."

The parallels between and the principles of the two gardens are too clear to ignore, and in the following pages you're invited into the fullness of all that Jesus accomplished in the garden to end all gardens. Ultimately, the garden of Eden finds its fulfillment in the garden of Gethsemane—and so, God willing, shall we. Because this is a journey about finding life.

HOW TO USE THIS BOOK

Finding Life is comprised of forty readings, appropriate at any time of the year, but designed specifically for use during Lent. The traditional Lenten observance excludes Sundays, which serve as an ongoing reminder of the resurrection. The first reading begins on Ash Wednesday, and the fortieth and final reading ends on Easter Eve.

Using *Finding Life* as a preparation for the triumph of Easter will be meaningful for the individual reader and groups as well, with daily application sections ideal for easily facilitating group study. Because faith must be much more than a mental exercise, each reading contains three sections after the narrative: listen, learn, and live.

LISTEN

The people of Berea, in the apostle Paul's time, "received the word with great eagerness, examining the

Scriptures daily, to see whether these things were so" (Acts 17:11). Any author's work is incomplete until compared with God's Word. When we listen to the Lord speak through Scripture, we compare our subject to the ultimate authority. During the listening time of each reading, we invite our gracious God to renew our minds through the Word, to speak to us anew, to prick our hearts and warm our souls.

One ancient means of listening to Scripture with new ears is what I call "circular reading." The Latin term for this is *lectio divina*, or sacred reading. The process is simple: Read the passage aloud, slowly; hold the words within your heart for a few seconds, much like savoring a rich bite of chocolate or the flavor of a charbroiled steak; and wait for God to press upon your conscious mind. Is there a phrase, word, or verse that especially moves you? You may want to write it in a notebook, keeping track of God's intimate whispers.

Repeat the process twice more, listening between each reading. The whisper may change; the phrase highlighted by God's Spirit may shift; but the important thing is to listen afresh to the passage. Finally, invite the Holy Spirit to show you what exactly to do with the Word this day.

LEARN

In this section, we learn from the thoughts of other authors, both current and classic. Because time is limited for all of us, these are sound bites, small nuggets to deepen our thinking and our application. They may provoke questions, clarify a point from the narrative, or expand on the subject matter. While we may not agree with the entire piece from which the work is excerpted, the Learn section is intended to make us ask questions and search for the application, to stretch us out of our comfort zone and into places of fresh, spring-green growth.

LIVE

Christianity was always intended to be practical, not simply intellectual, interesting, or stimulating. The Live section of each reading asks, essentially, "So what?" So we must not leave until we have moved closer to Gethsemane, until the truth begins to take root in our lives. This section can be used as a tool for prayer, reflection, journaling, and group discussion.

Søren Kierkegaard is noted as having said, "It is perfectly true, as philosophers say, that life must be understood backwards. But they forget the other proposition, that it must be lived forwards." Here, we take a closer look at how the subject impacts our own lives. This is the place where a mentor, if we had one, might ask us a deeply personal application question, one that makes us squirm but forces us to grow. If our lives were gardens— and gardens in Scripture are at times euphemisms for the soul—here we would look for brambles and briars, pests and parasites. Here we would deadhead, plucking off faded blooms to preserve energy for new blossoms. Here we create space for new growth. What difference does the garden make if it makes no difference in the way we live?

IN GROUP SETTINGS

To really find our lives, we need community. Not the red Jell-O fellowship of the old school potlucks, but a meat-and-potatoes meeting of people who care (or are at least curious) about their own journey with Christ and who care about us. *Finding Life* is designed for easy use in small groups, Sunday school classes, or for all-church study. There are seven weeks during Lent if a group meets Wednesday through Saturday; six weeks if a group meets on Monday or Tuesday. Each chapter is easily facilitated with no advance preparation necessary except to read through the week's readings.

At the back of this book, there is a small group guide to *Finding Life*. Also, visit www.wphresources.com/findinglife for a free, downloadable discussion guide divided into seven weekly sections.

IN BETWEEN

For the uncomfortable time being, we hover between two gardens, knowing that something is not quite right about this trek, something off on our compass. Much as we long for the perfection of Eden, still we resist pressing onward to the fulfillment of Gethsemane. But we can learn to flourish in between, learn to live with the tension of not quite, learn to live with what we don't fully understand, learn to lean toward hope while still in this land between.

PART 1

CREATION IN THE GARDEN

My grandparents, who had lived many adventures before marrying, and many more before bringing my father into the world, were ultimately tightly tied to the land, the cycles of weather, the seasons of rain and sun, rest and work, dormancy and growth.

When we rattled over the cattle guard to their farm each year at Easter, often dragging a long cloud of dust behind us, the cotton crop would be a short promise in all the fields. Like all gardens, just a hope. But in the late summer, the snowy-headed crops looked other-worldly, soft with surprising barbs snug in the womb of each boll.

The farm felt to my child's psyche like a paradise, and it whispered to some primal hunger for safety, beauty, and connection, as well as the satisfaction of rich earth yielding such prizes.

I see that now, but then I saw only the delights: the milk cow with steaming milk pinging against the cold, steel bucket; chickens scrabbling about their pen and brooding and clucking in the coop and the warm eggs they offered daily; cherry trees, giant party favors with millions of blooms; pecan trees, vegetable gardens, and the smoke house leaking its mouth-watering scent of cured meats. No ham or bacon has ever compared. My brother and I would stand outside the door and just breathe the rich, salty, smoky air, our mouths watering and tummies rumbling. I'm surprised that all the dogs in the county didn't line up at that door with hope in their eyes.

This was my Eden.

It was also the childish, romantic view of a visitor to the farm, one who partook of the treasures but not the toil.

Still, it imprinted on my young soul deep longing, nudging awake a lifelong, eternity-long ache.

Since then—perhaps for all of us is this true—so much of my journey has been a seeking, an attempt to recapture that innocent longing, then fulfilling it with my own rather handicapped wrestings, both literal and figurative, with soil, weeds, and zealous overplanting and undernurturing.

This is a journey about finding life, about the garden lost and the garden restored. And the endless creativity of the Creator, always beckoning us to wholeness.

REST IN THE GARDEN

Ash Wednesday

Our need to be needed preys upon our need for rest, and we lunge for telephones and tablets, neurotically check e-mail, texts, social media, and voice mail. We drag ourselves out of bed, slam the snooze button, and crawl back to the warm covers and five more minutes of oblivion. Fatigue hammers our nervous system and fills our blood with sludge. In a world where communication has become a waking nightmare, where instant accessibility increases our prospects of success as well as the looming nearness of insanity, the creation account reminds us of our priorities. Or at the very least, of God's.

In the order of creation, a *restful* night came before the working day, assuring us that rest is part of the natural rhythm and restoration of our fragmented lives. "And there was evening and there was morning, one day" (Gen. 1:5). In the Jewish calendar, the "day" begins at sundown, forcing followers to start each twenty-four-hour period with rest at the top. All else—work, relationships— proceeds from the time of rest.

This is telling in a world that spiritualizes exhaustion, wearing it as a merit badge. Not enough sleep and we perch on the brink of madness, of psychosis. We carry our weariness deep in our bones and settle for second-best when we work first and refuse to rest. We run on caffeine, adrenaline, and fear.

And yet, God set up a pattern in those first days of creation. There was evening and there was morning, the second day. Evening and morning, a third day. Evening and morning, a fourth day. All the way through until the seventh day of the first week, when we read, "By the seventh day God completed His work which He had done, and He rested on the seventh day from all His work which He had done. Then God blessed the seventh day and sanctified it, because in it He rested from all His work which God had created and made" (Gen. 2:2–3).

The Scriptures are not clear as to whether Adam and Eve waited for another week to roll around to test out the whole "day of rest" theory. Perhaps they would not have succumbed to temptation if they had observed a day of rest in between, a day to remember their priorities and Creator, and to trust. All we know is that ever since the expulsion from the garden, human beings have been on a fast track. Murder and mayhem fill the very next chapter of Genesis and lead us to Noah.

Amazingly, his name means "rest." Lamech, Noah's father, said, "This one shall give us rest from our work and from the toil of our hands arising from the ground which the LORD has cursed" (Gen. 5:29). Whether Noah would provide rest from farming because it's difficult to farm in a flood or because his life would be one of trust and obedience, I leave to you to decide. We do know, however, that Noah learned something about the meaning of his name and tried to live into it. Genesis 6:9 reads, "Noah was a righteous man, blameless in his time; Noah walked with God."

But the rest was short-lived. The very next generation filled its lives with shame, and the cycle of trust and toil again turned askew. They, too, toiled so much they could not trust, until God led them to the Promised Land. Thankfully, God has not left us without rest. As Warren Wiersbe wrote, "Noah means 'rest.' Mankind was in misery and longed for the promised Redeemer to come. He *has* come, and we can come to Him and find true rest."

Since the evacuation from Eden, we have grasped for the brass ring, only to learn that we clutch a painted, peeling, pockmarked piece of trash. We have underrated rest and overrated its second-best companion, work. What cataclysmic and colossal messes we make when we continue to live in a land without rest. Catastrophe, captivity, and chaos accelerate until we come to the Christ child, who grew up and urged us to put our necks with His in the yoke, that instrument of work, and find rest.

When we move through the garden of Gethsemane to the cross, we find that all our work is brokenness, and only the cross, only the crucified and risen Christ, brings rest. "Come to Me, all who are weary and heavy-laden, and I will give you rest" (Matt. 11:28).

"And the man has begun to be strong who has begun to know that, separated from life essential, that is God, he is weakness itself, but of strength inexhaustible if he be one with his origin," wrote George MacDonald in his book *Unspoken Sermons*. When we approach Christ, open our clenching fists, and lay down our armor of work and fatigue, we find again that oneness with Him, that irreplaceable rhythm of trust and toil.

And it was evening, and it was morning. Today. But rest today is another matter. Or is it?

The bright woman next to me at dinner talked animatedly about her faith and her decision to rest after twenty-six years of practicing law. "With the money I earned, I chose to buy myself time. I quit my job and began to think about the direction of my life." She smiled, clearly at peace with her choice. For her, listening time brought with it refreshing renewal; rest really did restore her tattered and battle-weary soul.

Not everyone can afford to quit work and reflect on life. Others at the table had taken two weeks out of their lives, vacation time for most of them, to fill themselves with Scripture and rest in that fullness. Rest, they were experiencing, clears the mind of rubble and weariness, sharpens focus, and purges panic and fuzzy thinking.

Does two weeks sound like too much? Not enough? What about resting from technology for a twenty-four-hour period? Decide which communication tool enslaves you the most, and cut the cord of dependency for a period of time. Julia Cameron, creativity specialist, suggests that word lovers rest for an entire week from words: all media, including books, newspapers, television, radio, and computer. And the "smart" part of your cell phone. Rest for a week from other people's words, and see if you don't find new words within; see if you don't find the Word of God once again living and active in the deep part of your soul.

And, as an additional leap of faith, what about tucking in at night at a decent time, shutting off all lights and nestling up to the One, the only One, who grants us rest? Maybe even going to sleep without a rash of rationale? As the inimitable G. K. Chesterton said,

> For those who study the great art of lying in bed there is one emphatic caution to be added. Even for those who can do their work in bed (like journalists), still more for those whose work cannot be done in bed (as, for example, the professional harpooner of whales), it is obvious that the indulgence must be very occasional. But that is not the

caution I mean. The caution is this: if you do lie
in bed, be sure you do it without reason or justi-
fication at all. . . . If a healthy man lies in bed, let
him do it without a rag of excuse; then he will get
up a healthy man. If he does it for some second-
ary hygienic reason, if he has some scientific
explanation, he may get up a hypochondriac.
(*Tremendous*)

Why do we rationalize or explain our need for rest?
Rest restores and reminds us of Augustine's wisdom: "You
have made us for yourself, and our heart is restless until it
rests in you." May you find your rest in God. Because first
there is evening, and then there is morning.

LISTEN

"Then in that day the nations will resort to the root
of Jesse, who will stand as a signal for the peoples; and
His resting place will be glorious" (Isa. 11:10).

"So there remains a Sabbath rest for the people of God.
For the one who has entered His rest has himself also rested
from his works, as God did from His" (Heb. 4:9–10).

LEARN

"The greatest act of faith that a man can perform is the
act that we perform every night. We abandon our identity,
we turn our soul and body into chaos and old night. We

uncreate ourselves as if at the end of the world: for all practical purposes we become dead men, in the sure and certain hope of a glorious resurrection" (Chesterton, *Lunacy*).

LIVE

How do you feel about rest, and when do you feel most tired? What keeps you from resting?

What part does rest play in your relationship with God?

Figure out the ideal number of hours you need for sleep. Then build your day and your to-dos from there.

2

LIGHT IN THE GARDEN

Some of my son's favorite music during toddlerhood came from *The Beginner's Bible*, sung by Jodi Bensen (of *The Little Mermaid* fame). The opening number sang the wonders of creation, the glories of those first days. My heart, too, always quickened when the words, "And God said, 'Let there be light!'" rang out.

God created light and split the night in two, a barrier that could never be trespassed for long. Such possibilities exist only in light, in the promise inherent in light: light illuminates, opens up, eliminates darkness, establishes freedom, eradicates fear. The absence of darkness is the presence of light, and God graciously gave us light. Darkness may allow for sleep, growth, and recovery— but light opens up the world. And the right amount of light is crucial for gardens to flourish.

One year, on a planting frenzy, I stuck hundreds of bulbs willy-nilly in the ground. In a yard easily half shaded—and the parts that weren't shaded were places one walks, not plants—finding a hundred slots for those bulbs was difficult. I decided to plant one of my favorite flowers, the French iris, next to hostas, thinking the hosta leaves would hide the iris leaves as those began to decay. But hostas love shade, primarily, and evidently irises thrive in sun, not shadow. When I remembered to look for the blooming plants in May, I found them sporting emaciated blooms and weak, pale, and nearly horizontal in their beds.

Degrees of light change everything, and light changes the world. God used light to set in motion growth, rest, and guidance. The absence of light meant it was time to trust, to rest in God's care, to allow in our own hearts that God will carry on with the world at least for a spell without us. When God's presence filled the tabernacle or temple, the glowing evidence was called the "Shekinah glory." Angels are introduced at times in the Scriptures with light, with "radiant beams." Lest we forget the serpent's ousting from Eden, we must remember that Satan masquerades as "an angel of light" (2 Cor. 11:14). God used light, in the form of a towering pillar of fire, to lead the way across the wilderness to the Promised Land. That's one big nightlight!

God continues to lead us with light, to show us the path, to guide us into truth. When we come to the New Testament, the book of John opens with, "In him was life, and that life was the light of all mankind. The light shines in the darkness, and the darkness has not overcome it. . . . The true light that gives light to everyone was coming into the world" (1:4–5, 9 NIV). The vital nature of this light grows even clearer when we consider the total eclipse of light on Calvary when Christ was crucified. Darkness fell upon the earth for three hours.

This light, the Christ-light, gives light to all, and changes the world.

Just look at the invention of the electric light by Thomas Edison in the 1800s. Not only did he give the gas companies (which controlled the only form of light except for candles and oil) a run for their money, he also ran the wires for a whole new world. Much of our technology today springs from those experiments and failures and ultimately the invention of the light bulb. From a world that ran on wicks and gas, our watches, phones, coffee pots, copy machines, and computer screens all light up.

Isn't it so of our souls? Our entire spiritual lives hang on Christ, who said of himself, "I am the light of the world. Whoever follows me will never walk in darkness, but will have the light of life" (John 8:12 NIV). Jesus is compared to the rising sun (Luke 1:78–79) and the morning star (2 Pet. 1:19), and in heaven, we'll have no need of the sun by day or the moon by night, "for the glory of God has illumined it, and its lamp is the Lamb. The nations will walk by its light, and the kings of the earth will bring their glory into it" (Rev. 21:23–24).

Without light, life is in danger. Light is being studied to treat chronic pain, autism, depression, and cancer, among other illnesses (Condor). Only a few minutes of sunlight each day triggers production of bone-strengthening vitamin D, and sunlight is crucial in combating rickets. High rates of depression, alcoholism, and suicide in Alaska, with its mere minutes of light in winter months, reinforce the importance of light.

Just as we can't live without light, we can't know true life without the light of Christ. In the Jewish culture, light represented God's holiness, and when the light of the glory of God shines in our hearts, when we become children of the light (John 12:36), we take up that light for others. It shines in and through us. Christ's own words clarify our position and the responsibility with the light entrusted to us: "You are the light of the world. A city set on a hill cannot be hidden. Nor does anyone light a lamp and put it under a basket, but on the lampstand, and it gives light to all who are in the house. Let your light shine before [others] in such a way that they may see your good works, and glorify your Father who is in heaven" (Matt. 5:14–16).

Christ, the Light of the World, transfers that flame to us. Too often, we hide the light, the brightness, the glory of God. Not wanting to seem boastful or proud, not wanting to stir comparison in others, we minimize God's light and action in our lives. But even as we have life in the light, so we share the life-light with others. And our lives, which were delivered from the domain of darkness, become a welcome invitation to others to join us in the light.

The light of Christ burns away the shadows of the soul, throwing wide the windows of our lives, that others might enter in and they, too, find light and life.

No wonder God said, "Let there be light" (Gen. 1:3).

LISTEN

"Because of the tender mercy of our God, by which the rising sun will come to us from heaven to shine on those living in darkness and in the shadow of death, to guide our feet into the path of peace" (Luke 1:78–79 NIV).

"So justice is far from us, and righteousness does not reach us. We look for light, but all is darkness; for brightness, but we walk in deep shadows. Like the blind we grope along the wall, feeling our way like people without eyes. At midday we stumble as if it were twilight; among the strong, we are like the dead. . . . Arise, shine, for your light has come, and the glory of the LORD rises upon you. See, darkness covers the earth and thick darkness is over the peoples, but the LORD rises upon you and his glory appears over you. Nations will come to your light, and kings to the brightness of your dawn" (Isa. 59:9–10; 60:1–3 NIV).

LEARN

"There is at the back of all our lives an abyss of light, more blinding and unfathomable than any abyss of darkness; and it is the abyss of actuality, of existence, of the fact that things truly are, and that we ourselves are incredibly and sometimes almost incredulously real. It is the fundamental fact of being, as against not being; it is unthinkable, yet we cannot unthink it, though we may sometimes be unthinking about it; unthinking and especially unthanking. For he who has realized this reality knows that it does far outweigh, literally to infinity, all lesser regrets or arguments for negation, and that under all our grumblings there is a subconscious substance of gratitude. That light of the positive is the business of the poets, because they see all things in the light of it more than do other men" (Chesterton, *Chaucer*).

LIVE

When do you shy away from the light? Why?

How have you cultivated time in the light of Christ?

In what way can you share that light today?

3

BEAUTY IN THE GARDEN

As our rental car rounded the curve and dipped into the park, my heart tried to hammer out of my rib cage. Incredible sculptures erupted from the ground in red-hued glory. No one but God could create such breath-stealing statues. But after hiking around in the baking sun, sweating and tromping through the clay-colored dust, I began to focus on my own discomfort. I grew numb to the glory. Isn't that a common frailty? Confronted by the majesty of God, all we can think of is the blister on our right foot.

Adam and Eve, it seems, also grew numb to the beauty of Eden. Too soon, they reached for the only item forbidden to them. Had Eden lost its attraction? Had they become bored so quickly? As they lost their footing in the garden soil, Adam and Eve began a life of longing—a longing for beauty that continues, unrequited, until we are once again united with God.

God's love is written across the entire sky, painting a complete picture of a loving, longing, wooing heart. The whole universe is a testimony, glowing, vivid, pulsing with the most amazing, living love letter. Gardens—beauty—appeal to us on many levels: the longing for beauty, for emotional connection, for life and love and future. More than anything, the endless beauty of God's creation cries out against our crowded lives, begging us to listen to those longings.

Beauty brings us into places of healing, as well as into God's presence. In *Gesundheit!*, the book written by Patch Adams and Maureen Mylander and brought to light by the Robin Williams movie *Patch Adams*, a patient and Patch are outside. The patient, Gareth, suffers from a type of arthritis that destroys the spine and all major joints in the body. He tells the story, "We watched a beautiful orange sunset in silence, and Patch turned to me and said, 'Do you have arthritis while you're watching this?' The question floored me. 'No, come to think of it, I don't'" (Adams).

Gareth hadn't noticed the absence of pain until Patch asked him; so, I think, we do not notice when the very hills cry out the presence of God. But when we notice, beauty eases pain and moves us toward God. Perhaps my own fascination with gardens has been rooted in the need to be increasingly aware of God's presence—loving, creative, and forgiving. Finding, seeking out those places—whether taking time to notice the giant trees outside the window or the intricate fabric of a dragonfly's wings—forces us out of a treadmill existence and into God's presence, into grace.

So much of the drama in Christ's life took place in beautiful settings: the baptism in the river, teaching His disciples on the Mount of Olives, speaking on the waterfront, all-night prayer in His favorite garden, burial and resurrection in a garden, His encounter with Mary Magdalene and the healing of her grief in the garden early in the morning.

Christ must have understood that beauty enhances intimacy, healing, and learning. Because He was always centered, always in touch with and attentive to God, maybe Jesus' strategic settings were for our sakes.

"The heavens declare the glory of God; the skies proclaim the work of his hands. Day after day they pour forth speech; night after night they reveal knowledge. They have no speech, they use no words; no sound is heard from them. Yet their voice goes out into all the earth, their words to the ends of the world" (Ps. 19:1–4 NIV).

In the words of the old hymn, "God, who touchest earth with beauty, make my heart anew; with thy Spirit recreate me, pure and strong and true" (Edgar). When God heals us of our deformity, the misshapenness of soul that comes from separation from God, beauty hedges and hems in our lives, and even as the heavens declare the glory of God, so the gardens of our lives beckon others to come and find healing.

As God began it all in Eden, God grants us another beginning in Gethsemane. The painful separation from God in Eden is put back together in Gethsemane. What began at a tree also ends at a tree, at the gruesome tree of the cross.

LISTEN

"I will heal their apostasy, I will love them freely, for My anger has turned away from them. I will be like the dew to Israel; he will blossom like the lily, and he will take root like the cedars of Lebanon. His shoots will sprout, and his beauty will be like the olive tree and his fragrance like the cedars of Lebanon. Those who live in his shadow will again raise grain, and they will blossom like the vine" (Hos. 14:4–7).

LEARN

"Have the unspoken yearnings of our soul been put there to draw us to the living God, a lover who dances into our dreams and schemes with the promise of fulfillment? Is He flirting with us when He sprays the sky with a multihued sunset or shatters the silence with frightening roars of thunderclap? Does He watch our wonder and wait to see if we're impressed as He leaps in the shadows for joy over His works? If so, what are we to do? How are we to respond to such magnificent exhibitions?" (Rhodes, *Taking*).

LIVE

Where are you most aware of the presence of God? How does scenery or beauty impact your soul?

What places of beauty are easily accessible to you? How often do you go there?

Where have you encountered beauty when none was visible?

PART 2

ONENESS IN THE GARDEN

I come to the garden alone
While the dew is still on the roses,
And the voice I hear falling on my ear,
The Son of God discloses.
And He walks with me, and He talks with me,
And He tells me I am His own;
And the joy we share as we tarry there,
None other has ever known.

—C. Austin Miles

How wonderful it would be to hear God's voice, intimate and distinct, definite with instruction and rich with love. What was it like for Adam and Eve to open their eyes and see God, to listen and actually hear God's voice? Now, our eyes are veiled, shadowed; we cannot see God face-to-face. We cannot physically walk with Jesus, as Mary Magdalene walked that dew-filled morning when Christ met her in the garden after Gethsemane's anguish, in the garden of the new tomb.

This frustrates me to no end. I want—or think I want, since I might not like what I hear—to hear God's voice, urgent and clear as a melody. I want marching orders, a sign to reveal exactly what to do next, where to go, and when to go. I want the towering pillar of fire to lead me, an enormous cloud to camp in front of me, rising and shifting only when it's safe to move on again. But I cannot hear, cannot see; the cataracts of humanity dim my vision so that I am not always aware that God is present, ever-loving and taking my hand along the path of life.

And there, I guess, my humanity shows up again—that base element that insists on answers, on guidance, and forgets about relationships. Our culture as a whole wants results; I'm no different. What I *want* to want is a relationship. Too often I want the benefits of that unbroken relationship without the accompanying responsibility.

After a year crammed with traveling and speaking, sometimes as often as fifteen times a month, I cried out to God: "I have no friends, no fellowship. This aloneness reveals my brokenness. I can't go on like this, nor is this pleasing to you." I wept after leaving my children and husband and was so exhausted upon returning that I could not enter gladly, easily, or fully into their lives.

This aloneness and lack of connection didn't just alarm me; it alarmed my covenant group, that group of godly women who asked insightful questions about my life, my faith, and God's call. Months had snuck by since

I'd attended our monthly meeting, and as I shared my soul, their loving, thoughtful silence deepened. A holiness seemed to fill the room. And they, too, echoed the voice of God in my innermost being, that voice ever calling, "Where are you?" It is not good, nor is it safe, to live in fissured fellowship. I not only failed to trust God's command to rest, but I also isolated myself from those whom God provided me for support.

This wasn't the Master Gardener's plan. Adam and Eve demonstrated for us first unbroken and then broken companionship; from the time of their creation in Eden through their exile, we recognize our own patterns of longing, choice, and their consequences. En route to Gethsemane, Jesus reestablished the possibility for unbroken fellowship in His life, death, and resurrection.

4

UNBROKEN IN EDEN

Unbroken fellowship with God originated with Adam and Eve, reflecting God's longing for intimate and continual communication with us. Their existence in Eden was protected, like an unborn infant in a mother's womb. Adam and Eve didn't know what they had. They had it made there in the garden, walking and talking with God. In their sinless state, they were able to look on God, something that we, as their heirs, cannot do in our fallenness, for God said, "No [one] can see Me and live" (Ex. 33:20).

Perhaps we all crave that connection, a craving that pulsed within Adam and Eve's hearts from the moment God formed them and breathed life into their nostrils. For us, the longing is easily disguised and fended off by our bustling, buying, constant list-making, and planning. This yearning still rears its head in our relationship-hopping, in the perfection-seeking drive within us that abandons friends when they disappoint us, in our fleeing of intimacy when the risk of being known threatens. If we listen to our lives, if we pay attention to the patterns we live out, we will identify this hunger: a deep soul-longing for a seamless reconnection with God.

God called; they heard. God freely walked about the garden of Eden. Imagine. God, the creator of all the earth, right on the other side of the hedges or strolling down the path lined with flowering trees, wanting time with you. Imagine knowing that you might run into God while rounding a bend or hear a heaven-filled whistling down the next row. Imagine anticipating seeing God at any moment. Did expectancy fill Adam and Eve? Did their hearts beat in a crazy, lopsided rhythm, some combination of the heartthrob of meeting a lover, the joy of seeing a best friend, and the happy clapping of a child seeing Daddy?

This is hard to picture in a world too preoccupied, self-focused, and tired to give much notice to even the visible, tangible people in our lives. We live numbed by the severing of relationships even as our bodies grow numb when a nerve is severed. The possibility of living in unbroken connection with anyone, let alone God, sounds far-fetched. And it might involve a great deal of work on our part, which means spending time, a scant commodity. But how appealing to imagine, to put ourselves in the place of Adam and Eve, to ponder the opportunity to watch for God on the path, expecting fully to see our Creator at the next juncture.

Surely in the same setting we would heed that call; surely we would hasten to God's side, join hands, listen, laugh, and intensely love this One who made and calls us.

But no. Experience shows that we, too, even given all those perks, would choose as Eve chose, respond as Adam responded.

LISTEN

"'You shall love the Lord your God with all your heart, and with all your soul, and with all your mind, and with all your strength. . . . You shall love your neighbor as yourself.' There is no other commandment greater than these" (Mark 12:30–31).

"For what I am doing, I do not understand; for I am not practicing what I would like to do, but I am doing the very thing I hate" (Rom. 7:15).

LEARN

"Connection is disappearing from modern life because a part of us wants it to. We want to get rid of the discomfort of the human moment. We want speed, efficiency, and control. Then we want rest and relaxation. The best way to achieve these goals is to deal with people as little as possible. They just get in the way!" (Hallowell).

LIVE

What keeps you from closeness in relationships—with God, with yourself, with friends? When do you recognize the craving for closeness? How do you avoid its fulfillment?

In a sentence, state your deepest longing for intimacy.

Are there people in your life who "just get in the way"? What is the best way to deal with them? What do you learn about yourself, considering them? And your reaction to them?

BROKEN IN EDEN

Seeing and hearing God walk about, they reached for something that looked like life but really contained death. For them . . . for us. Adam and Eve chose, perhaps unwittingly, perhaps not fully knowing the consequences of their choice. They chose knowledge, extending the right hand of fellowship to the fallen angel, Satan, in the form of a serpent. They preferred the power that comes with knowledge (eating from the Tree of Knowledge of Good and Evil) to the constant companionship of their friend and Creator.

Tempted by Satan's bait—"God knows that in the day you eat from it . . . you will be like God" (Gen. 3:5)—they snatched power over unbroken fellowship. And they broke forever the possibility of seeing God face-to-face, until the coming of the Lord Jesus, the promised Messiah.

This is coveting in its most naked, glaring form: It was Satan's sin in heaven before he fell; it was Adam and Eve's sin; it is mine. Wouldn't being *like* God be better than having to *rely on* God, especially now, when we can't even see God? We are uncomfortable with the unseen, with the walk by faith, with mystery and the unknown. Like Adam and Eve, we choose to *know*, to be like God in seizing control, shielding our vulnerabilities, withdrawing when people get too close or when intimacy requires being real.

The first couple listened to the wrong voices. Eve listened to the serpent's wiles. And to Adam, God said, "You have listened to the voice of your wife, and have eaten from the tree" (Gen. 3:17). Not to say men should never listen to their wives, simply that the primary voice we all heed must be God's. God's voice, the Word, is our ultimate sieve.

Our choices are too often death choices that separate us from hearing God, walking with God, talking with God, knowing that presence intimately. We listen to the wrong voice, heed the siren's call, and walk out of the life-giving garden of communion into a world of endings, of death.

After Adam and Eve fled Eden, the Scriptures recount the broken relationship. The exile was necessary, lest Adam "stretch out his hand, and take also from the tree of life, and eat, and live forever" (Gen. 3:22). Allowing Adam and Eve to live forever in brokenness and separation was intolerable to God; the exile from Eden meant that reestablishing oneness remained possible.

With hope we see Enoch, who walked with God, and then "he was not, for God took him" (Gen. 5:24; see also Heb. 11:5). In Genesis 5, a chapter constantly tolling the death song—"and he died," "and he died," "and he died"—Enoch's closeness with God brings a bloom of possibility to our journey toward the promised garden.

Moses' life, too, bears witness to the longing heart of God as Moses led the people out of Egypt toward the Promised Land. The Scriptures tell us, "Thus the LORD used to speak to Moses face to face, just as a man speaks to his friend" (Ex. 33:11). So holy was their relationship that Moses' face glowed from being in God's presence; he veiled the brilliance of his face when returning to the Israelites, lest they be burned (or convicted?) by the brightness. The possibility of oneness with God shines, as does the reality of brokenness. Moses begged God, "Show me Your glory!" God responded, "You cannot see My face, for no [one] can see Me and live!" (Ex. 33:18, 20). But God's longing, loving heart allowed Moses to be present when God passed by, shielding the servant-leader from death.

We know the end of that chapter in the Israelites' history: They refused to enter that next garden, the Promised Land, out of fear and forgetfulness. Fear often whispers through my own soul, even as it spread through the Israelites' camp like fog. I forget God's faithfulness and back away from God's promise to remain in me, to hold me, to provide for me. I sever connections even though loneliness shrouds me.

But Jesus waits. His life continually reminds us of the possibility of oneness with Him, of unbroken relationship.

LISTEN

"Behold, the LORD's hand is not so short that it cannot save; nor is His ear so dull that it cannot hear. But your iniquities have made a separation between you and your God, and your sins have hidden His face from you so that He does not hear" (Isa. 59:1–2).

LEARN

"If you want to change, you can. The best way to change is through changing your connections, deepening them, expanding them, maybe eliminating a few, pruning others, and fertilizing still others. You may develop a new friendship, or deepen your connection to beauty, or develop your connection to God, or make peace with a member of your family. There are many different ways to change through changing your connections" (Hallowell).

LIVE

Where do you see the yearning for connection and examples of its brokenness and its completion in your own life?

What do you choose in the place of intimacy? Where do you choose *to know* rather than to trust?

When have you felt God asking you to believe, to trust God in the unseen rather than the facts, which are seen?

6

JESUS WITH GOD

Jesus' fellowship with God was unbroken both in heaven and on earth. He modeled unbroken communion with God by living in human form in 100 percent dependence on God. He didn't rely on His being wholly God; rather, on earth He "emptied Himself" (Phil. 2:5–8) and became fully human, living as a human being like us but in total reliance on God. I love reading Christ's conversations with others in Scripture; how often He responded to the thoughts and whisperings of others though He didn't hear their audible questions or condemnation. Because of His constant dialogue with God, because He always listened with His heart to the God's voice, Jesus addressed people's thoughts with piercing accuracy.

Jesus depended entirely on God. This is why in that night of darkness and soul-splitting prayer in the garden He could plead with God to take the cup of suffering away from Him, but then say, "Not My will, but Yours" (Luke 22:42). Until that moment of utter abandonment on the cross—"My God, My God, why have You forsaken Me?" (Matt. 27:46)—Jesus' relationship with God was never fractured. Only when Christ took upon himself the separation that is the root of all our sin, only then was God's intimacy broken with His only Son. To save us, to provide for us the possibility of fellowship with God, God the Son severed His own profoundly intimate relationship with God the Father and God the Spirit.

Who can know the agony God experienced in those hours of separation between Son, Father, and Spirit? The Scriptures remain mute; we can only touch the edges of that rib-squeezing grief. And here, too, we can almost feel the intensity of God's heartbreak at our separation, when the darkness of sin hides His face from us.

Imagine that moment when Jesus burst forth from the clutches of death itself—how the trumpets must have blown in heaven. What rejoicing, what a celebration—the One who was dead is now alive! What heavenly hymns must have heralded Jesus' victory! He rose and was reunited immediately in spirit with God and in body with His beloved friends on earth. When He returned to heaven, Jesus left behind His Spirit, that we would never again be disconnected from Him.

Never again can death separate us from God—neither can life! Because Christ bore the agony of separation for us, we need never be apart again.

LISTEN

"For I am convinced that neither death, nor life, nor angels, nor principalities, nor things present, nor things to come, nor powers, nor height, nor depth, nor any other created thing, will be able to separate us from the love of God, which is in Christ Jesus our Lord" (Rom. 8:38–39).

LEARN

Communion with God—that deep-felt, unbroken bond of love—steadied Jesus, moved Him along the rugged path to Golgotha, sustained Him in the garden of Gethsemane, and allowed Him to be pounded to the cross. Only when Christ took on the sins of the world was the bond of love broken. For our sakes He broke that communion and now, in resurrection for our sakes, reestablishes the bond through the power of the Holy Spirit. May that bond of loving communion keep us both steady and loving.

LIVE

When are you most separated from God?

When have you experienced God reaching out to you, calling you by name, establishing a connection with you?

What keeps you from an immediate response?

7

BROKEN RELATIONSHIPS

Relationships, whether with God or with others, begin to break down when we overload them with unrealistic expectations. The disciples' expectations of Jesus—that He would be a reigning monarch like other political leaders, that He would deliver them immediately from physical oppression, that His power would look like the power of other kings—kept them from truly listening to what Jesus told them about himself. Ultimately, they fled at His death, denying Him and fracturing their relationship, because they expected something far different than what He delivered.

Our relationships break down when we expect others to be what they are not and cannot accept them for who they truly are. As a newlywed and later as a pastor's wife, I expected that my husband's primary role would be to meet all my needs: He should be my lover, confidant, best friend, spiritual advisor, physical trainer; he should also be good with a checkbook. Without processing our own needs and expectations in relationships, we're in danger of sinking them.

In our churches, we often see the fracturing of fellowship due to unrealistic expectations. Disunity in the church may be caused by a need to feel valued and valuable and may look like the disciples jostling for the seat at Jesus' right hand. Rather than work at staying in relationship, at the first sign of discord we may jump ship, leave the church, and drop out of the life of faith because someone didn't prove to be perfect or had more gifts than we had. Unity with one another is a sign of our oneness with God. This fracturing of relationships in the church is another sign of our brokenness and separation. Rather than giving cause for judgment of another, it demonstrates our need to live in constant communication with God.

Relationship fractures also occur when we give others false impressions of ourselves. In college I pretended to exercise for the fun of it, though I can't say I ever experienced a runner's high. There is nothing remotely fun about exercise as far as I can tell. When Rich and I met and married several years later, I had never gotten past the fatigue stage of exercise, or the "I can't stand this" phase, but my new husband couldn't know that. He thought he was exchanging rings with someone who loved working out, and we lifted weights together (twice), hiked, and biked. In spite of good companionship, on my list of enjoyable activities, exercise falls below cleaning sewer lines. This was a blow for Rich, and he felt deceived.

False impressions may stem from not truly knowing who we are and from not experiencing ourselves as beloved by God, *as is*. I didn't mean to deceive; I just never thought about the "whys" of my actions and the impressions those actions gave. Other uglier examples of false expectations and false impressions exist, but the point is, even in minor instances, these cause relationship fractures.

Fractures also develop when we ignore a relationship. We can go for days or even weeks without really talking to one another. James and Kathryn, married twenty years, found out the hard way when they went into business together. They made great business partners; their gifts were perfectly compatible for building and running a business, but soon the business talk took over their entire home life so that they were no longer married emotionally.

Sometimes parents learn this when suddenly faced with time alone together after years of talking only about child-rearing details. The empty nest often empties out even more when the couple realizes they no longer know one another.

Susan and Karen were the best of friends, next-door neighbors, and coffee companions until a job transfer shoved a long-distance wedge between them. The space between conversations lengthened until they corresponded only with a note at Christmas, and then, finally, even those token letters stopped. Relationships are difficult to maintain and improve without time together.

An imbalance in give-and-take can also create problems. If a relationship seems like a monologue to you, is it really a friendship? If, for instance, Brad does all the talking and Allen does all the listening, where is the intimacy? If Nolan always helps his buddies and their families move or fixes their cars or plumbing, and they don't help him when he needs help, where is the balance? Always giving, never receiving—or the opposite—shows imbalance.

This is true for our relationships with one another and our relationship with God. I used to dislike prayer and didn't feel particularly close to God; then I realized that most of my prayer life was me telling God what to do, how, and for whom. I filed away my prayer lists and filled myself up with God's Word, and waited. I paid attention. I loved God by ceasing my jabbering, controlling, and working. And, amazingly, I became more aware of God's love for me. Then, carrying concerns about others to God, I freely released those burdens.

As we grow in our ability to recognize relationship blocks and examine our own responsibilities in their creation, we're better able to sustain those relationships. Living in constant communion with others and with God can't be impossible, or Jesus couldn't have demonstrated that intimacy. As we listen more, we will recognize more and more the voice of God speaking to us, in silence, in the Word, and through others, for sheep know the Shepherd's voice.

LISTEN

"My sheep hear My voice, and I know them, and they follow Me; and I give eternal life to them, and they will never perish; and no one will snatch them out of My hand. My Father, who has given them to Me, is greater than all; and no one is able to snatch them out of the Father's hand. I and the Father are one" (John 10:27–30).

LEARN

"Our dignity is that we are children of God, capable of communion with God, the object of the love of God—displayed to us on the cross—and destined for eternal fellowship with God. Our true value is not what we are worth in ourselves, but what we are worth to God, and that worth is bestowed upon us by the utterly gratuitous love of God. All our lives should be ordered and conducted with this dignity in view" (Temple).

LIVE

Which fracturing elements do you most often use? Why?

When have you overcome some of those relationship fractures?

How is the Shepherd calling, leading you toward Him?

8

LISTENING TO THE VOICE

After my covenant group so graciously spoke to me in love, I knew the truth. I had been speaking in ministry so often that I spent little time listening. It's difficult to do both at the same time, and all the speaking and its troubling companion—incessant motion—had drowned out the song in my heart. One Monday as my seasonal speaking commitments neared their end, deep joy welled up. Over and over the words to Keith Green's song "There Is a Redeemer" rushed up from my soul and burst out of me.

When our eight-year-old tore into the house after school, he braked in surprise. "Mom, I didn't know you could sing." This from a child to whom I sang endlessly while rocking, nursing, and cuddling. I smiled, hugged him, and ruffled his poky hair, but my heart was sad. Minutes later the song returned, and again, Josh exclaimed, his face filled with wonder, "I just didn't know you could sing!"

The sadness took over then, tightening my throat with grief. Later I bowed before God. Stress, exhaustion, and busyness had extinguished the song for so long that my children didn't even know that sometimes music lived in me. What dangerous evidence of broken fellowship, living one life in public and a different life in private. Joy is one of the first losses when we stop listening, and as much as I love this portion of my calling, life had been decidedly joyless.

As I responded to God's pressure and presence with a string of "I'm sorries" to speaking invitations, lightness filled me. I bounced around the house for days like a helium balloon. Writing became a nurturing time with God again, and my energy and laughter around my family grew.

God had handed me the microphone hundreds of times during that season, taking me around the country so others might hear God's voice through my teaching (not singing). And then, for a spell, God seemed to want me to limit my own words in order to better listen, to better practice the unbroken fellowship for which I long. No, the speaking wasn't sin; the issue was obedience to God's call. When I picked up the microphone again and returned to an itinerant circuit, it was with a different energy and attentiveness to God's voice.

For all of us, perhaps obedience means less of our own voice that we might come to know God's voice all the better and that our loved ones, too, might come to know and love that voice, because they hear it as a joyful melody line through our own lives. Then, in all situations, those words ring with truth and power.

He speaks, and the sound of His voice
Is so sweet, the birds hush their singing,
And the melody that He gave to me
Within my heart is ringing.

And He walks with me, and He talks with me,
And He tells me I am His own;
And the joy we share as we tarry there,
None other has ever known.

—C. Austin Miles

LISTEN

"These things I have spoken to you so that My joy may be in you, and that your joy may be made full. . . . But now I come to You; and these things I speak in the world so that they may have My joy made full in themselves" (John 15:11; 17:13).

"What we have seen and heard we proclaim to you also, so that you too may have fellowship with us; and indeed our fellowship is with the Father, and with His Son Jesus Christ. These things we write, so that our joy may be made complete" (1 John 1:3–4).

LEARN

"I have community with others and I shall continue to have it only through Jesus Christ. The more genuine and the deeper our community becomes, the more will everything else between us recede, the more clearly and purely will Jesus Christ and his work become the one and only thing that is vital between us. We have one another only through Christ, but through Christ we do have one another, wholly, and for all eternity" (Bonhoeffer, *Life*).

LIVE

What have you been asked to relinquish?

Where have you struggled in your choices of intimacy versus brokenness?

What can you begin to do to mend a fractured relationship?

PART 3

DARKNESS IN THE GARDEN

Our son read aloud from the camp application, "How do you feel about the dark?" He paused, pen in hand, scrunching up his face. Then, quickly, he scrawled in the blank with fourth-grade boy handwriting, "Not afraid of it." This from the guy who once wouldn't walk into a room without a light on, who needed accompaniment into any and all dark places. But somehow, with the form in front of him, he was able to look ahead, into the dark, and gird up his soul and forge ahead. "Not afraid of it."

I am not so brave. I am afraid of the dark, of the darkness within me—darkness that is the very worst of me, the ugliest parts of me that I hide, with varying degrees of success, from others—and darkness outside of me. Too often, it feels as if I have no control over either darkness.

Once, members of our church went on a mission trip to an inner-city church. We, a sheltered church in between farmland and suburb, immersed ourselves in the heart of darkness in Chicago. We hammered, sawed, cleaned, painted, laughed, sang, and worshiped. And then, sur-rounded by thick emotional darkness, tried to sleep in the sanctuary with the "crime lights"—the floodlights that illuminated any movement outside the church—the sirens, and the uneasy night noises.

Restless on my pew, with both comfort and the oblivion of sleep evading me, I decided to creep downstairs to their fellowship hall to journal. I felt my way down the steps, running my hand along the wall, and halted in the total blackness on the last step. Where was the light switch? Across the room. I plunged into the darkness and rushed for the light, flipping it on.

I screamed and leapt into a chair. Thousands of roaches swarmed across the floor, at home in the dark, panicked by the light. Terror jangled every nerve in my body. I crouched on the chair and tucked my bare feet underneath me, hugging my knees. Those black bugs with their crunchy shells made me shudder. Their icky, germ-carrying, darkness-loving bodies encapsulated everything I feared.

Bad things happen in the dark. Whether looking at temptation, deceit, violence, nighttime, or night noises, darkness is a breeding ground. And our gardens are no exception.

9

TEMPTATION IN THE GARDEN

Temptation in the first garden is well documented. The lure of that which is off limits has tempted everyone from the first couple down through the generations. It reminds me of a child in a room filled with new toys and a cash register full of money. "Play with anything. It's yours. Every single item here. Oh, but leave the cash register alone." The child looks around, and the forbidden looms larger than life, more appealing than anything else in the whole world.

Temptation: to entice to do wrong by promise of either pleasure or gain. Satan knew his targets, knew their weakness. Knows ours. In a world where a two-buck lottery ticket can make us millionaires, where the promise of easy gain through gambling snares many; in a world where insider trading and the stock market's ascending numbers beckon and then take a nation down with them, the temptation to do wrong is immense. In this world, this brave new world, pleasure often feels like the adrenaline-rushing temptation of risk, so taking risks—

whether shoplifting's thrill or trying to entice another by look or by crook of a finger—scores big on the charts.

Adam and Eve, lured by the promise of being like God, becoming little gods, bought into the lie. And our susceptibility to temptation, to illicit gain, to self-serving pleasure, has not decreased through history. Everyone is fair game, including Jesus.

Though the wilderness could hardly be called a garden, Jesus' "ordination" ceremony consisted of forty days of temptation by Satan. The adversary's forte is twisting the Word, taking it out of context, editing it to suit his own purposes. But Jesus, the Author, knew the Word in its entirety and withstood. Jesus came against every temptation, every word from the serpent's mouth, battling it with the Word of God.

Still, Satan would not desist. He trailed Jesus, tempting Him at every turn. In fact, the Scriptures say that Jesus was "tempted in all things as we are, yet without sin" (Heb. 4:15). At any point, Jesus could have succumbed to the adulation, to the temptation to use His power in a self-serving way. But His connection with God enabled Him to stay faithful, to withstand, to resist shortcuts promising easy gain. In the garden of Gethsemane, Jesus sweat drops of blood, earnestly beseeching God, "Take this cup from me" (Luke 22:42 NIV). Tempted to circumvent His calling, He battled it with prayer by connecting to the power and presence of His Abba.

The next day in court, Jesus could have polished His image. For most of us, the temptation to look good is powerful. But Jesus, in Luke's crucifixion account, did not shine His reputation before Pilate or Herod, even though Herod was "greatly pleased" to see Jesus, because "he hoped to see him perform a sign of some sort" (Luke 23:8 NIV). The assembly before Pilate told an outright lie about Jesus with their accusation, "He opposes payment of taxes to Caesar" (23:2 NIV), but our Lord responded only with silence.

And poor Peter—he tagged along with Christ near the riverfront, when the Lord had instructed him to go catch a fish, take out the coin he would find in its mouth, and "render to Caesar the things that are Caesar's" (Matt. 22:21). Peter knew the truth, and could have opposed the accusation, I suppose. Christ's tools against temptation—prayer and knowing the Word of God, which is sharper than a two-edged sword (see Heb. 4:12)—were available to Peter and are available now to us. But disciples, then and now, are vulnerable to the serpent of temptation.

In the garden of Gethsemane, when Jesus rose from pleading with the Father, "May this cup be taken from me. Yet not as I will, but as you will" (Matt. 26:39 NIV), He found His companions of three years—people with whom He had built His life, whom He had tutored daily—sleeping. Not once, but three times.

What patience and grace Jesus offered the disciples in their time of tempting, especially in light of His own fervent wrestling just beyond their knapsacks. Because He fought against and won over temptation, His words carried credibility and power. Jesus knew that the disciples couldn't win over temptation without prayer. Did the disciples see the blood streaking His face from His grappling? Without prayer, temptation would win.

But Jesus also knew they were exhausted with sorrow, and fatigue and sorrow leave us vulnerable and lead us into temptation. Yet the tried-and-true weapon to combat these remains the same: finding that ultimate rest in God. In Jesus' words, "Watch and pray" (Matt. 26:41 NIV).

Our temptations seem trivial in light of the Scripture records of Jesus' dark travail in the garden. His tolerance for the disciples' sleeping through His own trial and for our struggles today is sobering considering the meaning of the original New Testament word for *temptation*. It's rooted in a word meaning "to pierce." We have not yet resisted to the point of shedding blood, yet our every temptation pierces both our soul and Jesus. He was "pierced through for our transgressions" (Isa. 53:5).

Jesus' strategy remains the same for us. In temptation, when we're seduced by illegitimate pleasure or ill-gotten gain or even seemingly harmless thrill seeking or image shining, our weapons are tried and true. When sorrow and fatigue hook bony fingers toward us, urging us to indulge in sleep or escape rather than war against the enemies in the garden, we know the truth. Prayer and the

Word of God enable us to withstand any temptation. In these very tools we find Christ himself: "Since He Himself was tempted in that which He has suffered, He is able to come to the aid of those who are tempted" (Heb. 2:18).

This is such a miracle that in the immediacy of our temptation, in the darkest wrestling of our souls, Christ is present.

LISTEN

"For we do not have a high priest who cannot sympathize with our weaknesses, but One who has been tempted in all things as we are, yet without sin. Therefore let us draw near with confidence to the throne of grace, so that we may receive mercy and find grace to help in time of need" (Heb. 4:15–16).

LEARN

"Temptations can be useful to us even though they seem to cause us nothing but pain. They are useful because they can make us humble, they can cleanse us, and they can teach us. All of the saints passed through times of temptation and tribulation, and they used them to make progress in the spiritual life. Those who did not deal with temptations successfully fell to the wayside. . . . Peace is not found by escaping temptations, but by being tried by them. We will have discovered peace when we have been tried and come through the trial of temptation" (à Kempis).

LIVE

How would you define *temptation*? When are you most susceptible to it? In what settings?

What effect do fatigue and sorrow have on your ability to withstand temptation?

How have you successfully battled temptation?

10

DECEIT IN THE GARDEN

With galling *savoir faire*, deceit sidled into Eden. Smooth and winsome, the serpent promised Eve that she wouldn't die but rather would become like God.

"The serpent deceived me, and I ate" (Gen. 3:13). Eve's blame slid out like lines in a well-rehearsed play. Did they feel the effect in their bodies and souls as soon as the forbidden fruit touched their palates? Did Adam and Eve know the truth immediately? That in fact, had they remained constant, they would never have known death? But now, in spite of those treacherous words, "You surely will not die" (3:4), they had done that very thing. While their bodies remained alive, their spirits died, separated instantly from the God of life, the God who would never die.

The serpent deceived the first couple, and they passed on a heritage of deceit. A few verses later, their son Cain was jealous of his brother Abel, who brought an offering more pleasing to God. Cain's face grew long and sullen, and God said, "Why are you angry? Why is your face downcast? If you do what is right, will you not be accepted? But if you do not do what is right, sin is crouching at your door; it desires to have you, but you must rule over it" (Gen. 4:6–7 NIV).

But Cain ignored God's warning—and the promise that sin needn't rule over him—and lured Abel into the field, killing him. God asked, "Where is your brother Abel?" Cain refused to answer the question. "I don't know. . . . Am I my brother's keeper?" (4:9 NIV).

As though he didn't understand the ramifications of his own self-deception, as though he didn't know the truth—this is the kind of deception to which we are all vulnerable. Pretending ignorance, we claim that we are innocent. "I didn't know. I didn't think. Is this my job? No one told me." This sort of deception shirks responsibility and keeps us out of the garden. The deceit of blame—blaming another, blaming a substance, blaming a circumstance—is an attempt at rationalization that avoids growth and allows weeds to choke our souls.

Not long after Cain left us his legacy, we find Isaac's son Jacob, given the unfortunate name meaning "the supplanter." Living up to—or rather down to—his name, he tricked his brother Esau, then his father, and stole his brother's birthright as a firstborn son. He struck a deal for a wife, and Rebekah's father tricked him, substituting his elder but less-beautiful daughter Leah in place of the one bargained for. Only seven more years of labor for Jacob to earn the rights to the wife of his choice. The legacy of deceit and trickery bleeds throughout the centuries.

Judas has gone down in history as the most infamous traitor, so much so that we say, "You're a real Judas" when we believe someone to have turned against us. Though Judas never deceived Jesus, he deceived their companions because the lure of money and power deceived him. Kissing Jesus on the cheek, he turned and handed Him over to the guards. (See Luke 22:39–53.) The reality of Judas's betrayal sunk in soon after the cold silver filled his hands. He had committed treason toward the only man on record who called him "friend." The poison injected his soul, and he rushed out in despair and took his own life. Even his betrayal of the very Son of God, I believe, could not have separated Judas from God for all eternity if only he had understood the saving, forgiving grace and love of his Lord. The Man who could forgive a thief hanging at His side on a stark cross, who could forgive Peter after his multiple denials of Him—this Jesus was capable of redeeming even the traitorous Judas.

And Peter. Peter, the pet of parents of prodigals, the darling of those who raised strong-willed, impetuous children, because he ultimately received Christ's forgiveness put himself into a position of trust and obedience, and faithfully sowed the seeds of Christianity. But it was a painful, disappointing journey pre-cross. Peter's problem leading up to those dark moments in Gethsemane was his own deception: about himself, his own faithfulness, his own abilities, and his own dark spaces of soul. Peter didn't know he had such capacity to deny Christ; he couldn't envision such treasonous behavior. "Lord, with You I am ready to go both to prison and to death!" (Luke 22:33). But Christ knew, foretold it, and with grace upheld Peter: "But I have prayed for you, that your faith may not fail" (22:32).

We bear striking resemblance to Adam and Eve. Certainly we're not unlike Jacob, Judas, and Peter. For do we not commit treason, like Judas, when we hand over Jesus to the world by our own sinfulness, our actions that speak not of love, but of power, envy, lust? Don't we betray Christ when we remain silent in the face of another's pain or passive in the face of injustice; when we fail to love, forgive, and welcome others? We exchange our relationship with the Lord of life for the few coins of self-pity, pouting, or revenge. These power tools don't lead us to God; they separate us from God, even as they drill holes in our relationships with others. Like Peter, we just don't know the depths of our capacity for betrayal, but Christ, who prayed His way through Gethsemane and the cross, does. And yet, for us, too, Jesus says, "But I have prayed for you, that your faith may not fail."

LISTEN

"If we say that we have no sin, we are deceiving ourselves and the truth is not in us. If we confess our sins, He is faithful and righteous to forgive us our sins and to cleanse us from all unrighteousness" (1 John 1:8–9).

LEARN

"We should deal with the betrayer not as an enemy, but as a friend. At the core of the psyche of the betrayer is not an evil spirit, but failed love. Betrayers do not need forgiveness that issues from the love of another, but the restoration of a love within themselves that has gone awry. This is why it is so difficult for those who have betrayed others to be received back into fellowship through repentance and forgiveness. For betrayal tears away the flesh of fellowship and friendship, leaving only the visible skeleton of love's despair. This is too terrible to look upon, and too revealing of the fear that hides in our own love, for us to tolerate. . . . With God's love there is no insecurity and ambivalence. God's love has no seed of betrayal, as evidenced by His faithfulness toward Israel in their disobedience. The love of Jesus has no element of betrayal, as evidenced by His faithfulness even toward those disciples who fled and the soldiers who nailed Him to the cross" (Anderson).

LIVE

Silence, passivity, envy, lust, power, self-pity, revenge—these are faces of treason, of self-deception. Which of these get between you and others? Between you and God?

What is your most striking experience of self-deception? When have you been deceived or felt betrayed by another? How do you react to betrayal or deception?

When have you deceived or betrayed another? How did you find your way back to the presence of Christ, or how did Christ find you again?

11

VIOLENCE IN THE GARDEN

Violence is almost a curse word in Christian circles; the air swirls with sharp intakes of breath when discussing the possibility of violence. It is the hushed, unspoken word. We think of battered wives and their vows of silence because of shame, and we refuse to mention violence in our churches and homes. Yet violence isn't limited to physical roughness and resultant harm. Violence is akin to the word *violate*, which means to break or disregard, and violence and violation subtly destroy many in the body of Christ and in this world. This violence is rooted in the broken paradise of the first garden.

Violence in Eden? Such a juxtaposition—violence and paradise—even the disrupted paradise we see in the Scriptures. And yet in Eden we find a different kind of violence, a violence that murders the spirit, a violence of soul that defaces the image of God in another. In Eden, not only did Adam and Eve violate their relationship with one another, but they also brought violence into the garden when they broke God's plan for them. Their disregard for their loving Creator's provisions brutally ushered in a cycle that eclipsed the image of God in the following generations. They violated their oneness with God in an action that resulted in instant spiritual death and the ramifications spread like sound waves into our own lives.

Violence easily hides its brutal face. Farmers sometimes had "fills" on their property into which they dumped glass, tin cans, and other unburnable items. They would then cover the trash with soil. "Throw that in the fill," my grandmother would tell me. After years passed, these fills weren't visible, but underneath the cover of dirt and grass, the pieces of glass and rubble would gradually work their way to the surface, one day cutting a bare foot or animal paw.

Anita's life was like the hidden fill. No one in her church knew that during her childhood she daily witnessed violence between her parents. By the time she married, this timid woman had either heard through closed doors or personally watched, terrified on the sidelines, thousands of instances of physical, emotional, and spiritual violence. No one knew her secret until the trauma worked its way to the surface of her life, her marriage, and her family.

But that's the overt violence. Not-so-obvious violence includes violation of another's soul, the breaking of spirit and of will; this, too, is violence. The force that effaces a child's natural curiosity and creativity and spontaneity— this is violence. In *The Joy Luck Club*, Amy Tan speaks of this violation: "For all these years I kept my mouth closed so selfish desires would not fall out. . . . All these years I kept my true nature hidden, running along like a small shadow so nobody could catch me. . . . I did not lose myself all at once. I rubbed out my face over the years washing away my pain, the same way carvings on stone are worn down by water. . . . I also remember what I asked . . . so long ago. I wished to be found."

I have encountered in myself a violence that could wound, even kill—a violence that, unleashed, would destroy. This darkness lurks in us all, from the death-row prisoner to the circumspect businessperson to the carefree child to the person in the seat next to us on Sunday.

And what of the violence of word or deed that maims? We destroy the image of God when we mock, belittle, or hold up to ridicule or scorn. Name-calling is violence. When someone referred to me in my husband's presence as "the wife," I felt violated, reduced to a role and minimized. I wasn't a person. What about God? When we refer to Him as "the Man Upstairs" or "the Boss," is that a betrayal or undermining His personal involvement in our lives?

The churning of violence continues, leading us to the violence in Gethsemane.

Beginning with that kiss of betrayal, violence robs the garden of Gethsemane of peace, as Jesus' painful prayer comes to fruition. A "multitude" invades the quiet place, a crowd of "chief priests and officers of the temple and elders" (Luke 22:52). They emanated violence, otherwise how did the disciples immediately perceive what would happen? They asked, "Lord, shall we strike with the sword?" (22:49). And impetuous Peter sliced off the ear of the high priest's slave.

Jesus' response was acute: "Stop! No more of this" (22:51). He refused to counteract violence with violence and touched the man's ear and healed him. Jesus delivered a pointed question to the armed crowd: "Have you come out with swords and clubs as you would against a robber? While I was with you daily in the temple, you did not lay hands on Me" (22:52–53). That the violence came from the hands of the religious establishment, the official rule-watchers, shouldn't surprise us. Any time we separate ourselves from a steady relationship with God, we're so vulnerable to darkness.

The brutality Jesus endured while in custody turns my stomach. I want to skim over Luke's account of the beating, spitting, and mocking, but I can't. For violence is intimately woven into each of us, and we, in the same place, would perhaps choose the same ugly, dehumanizing acts. Tricia McCary Rhodes, quoting Alexander Whyte, said, "You will understand that spitting scene that night when God lets you see your own heart" (*Contemplating*).

Jesus' crucifixion is the ultimate act of violence — against humanity, perfection, and the voice of God. And

Jesus' response, the words of our gracious and redeeming Lord, breaks my heart and convicts me. Even as they hammered spikes into His flesh and hoisted His battered, bleeding body into the air, Jesus pleaded with God: "Father, forgive them; for they do not know what they are doing" (Luke 23:34). Violence shredded His back, blood dripped from His wounds, bruises and welts throbbed. But Jesus, our Jesus, said, "Forgive them; for they do not know what they are doing."

Perhaps my heart breaks because I, too, have shredded flesh with words; I have hammered spikes with vengeful thoughts; I have drawn blood with a glare. But the voice of Christ returns, over and over. "Forgive them. Forgive them. Forgive them."

Even violence finds redemption on a barren hill called Golgotha.

LISTEN

"He was oppressed and He was afflicted, yet He did not open His mouth; like a lamb that is led to slaughter, and like a sheep that is silent before its shearers, so He did not open His mouth" (Isa. 53:7).

LEARN

"Precious Redeemer . . . what can I say to you—you who have been spit upon and ridiculed. You whose face is now misshapen by the blows of sinners. You who bleed, and fall . . . and yet utter not a word. I cry, but my tears seem a trivial testament to the torment you endure. What can I say? Nothing. Silent sorrow is my only recourse. I pray your heart can sense my grief" (Rhodes, *Contemplating*).

LIVE

What kind of "fill" do you hide on the property of your soul? What junk do you hide there and why? And when does glass or a rusty sharp metal piece erupt and hurt you or another?

When have you encountered violence (or its potential) within yourself? With others? Consider not only physical violence, but emotional and spiritual violence as well.

How have you responded? How has God responded?

12

NIGHT IN THE GARDEN

As a child, watching the television show *Dark Shadows* did very little to ease my fear of nighttime. Rather, it heightened my awareness of the encroaching dark. Every siren shattering the night meant a burglar skulked outside my window. Each creak shot ominous warnings through my system. The moon hanging in the sky befriended me, and I learned to love turning on a light and reading, even studying, in the middle of the dark night. I greeted mornings with joy because that meant night had ended.

God separated the night from the day, making each period finite. "The earth was formless and void, and darkness was over the surface of the deep, and the Spirit of God was moving over the surface of the waters." God created light, approved it, and then "separated the light from the darkness. God called the light day, and the darkness He called night" (Gen. 1:1–2, 4–5). The act of naming has a sense of mastery to it. When Adam was given the privilege of naming all the animals, it was a sign of his dominion. So when we hear God giving the darkness a name, night, we know that He has exercised His authority over the night. This is comforting news to the small child who still crouches within us, riddled with fear at the things that go bump in the night.

Not only did day and night, light and dark, exist in Eden; night also stooped outside at the gate, awaiting admittance to the hearts of God's beloved. When they threw open the door for doubt and greed, saying yes to the serpent, Adam and Eve opened themselves up to the night, casting out the light of God from within. And dark became, rather than simply a time of rest and some sweet bedtime stories, a time of soul darkness. From then until the New Testament, we can trace the night.

Night takes many forms. It can mean the absence of moral values, a period of darkness emotionally or spiritually, or a period of dreary inactivity or affliction. Sounds like the Israelites' journey as they drag through the pages of history. Idolatry, war, wandering, sin, loss of faith—all these speak of night. The moral decay of society crowds out the light and throws us into night. Depression and anger, the darker emotions also suggest the night.

But even as morning faithfully brought the ending of night in my childhood, so the coming of the Son of Man brought the ending of night to the darkness of our lives. The wise men saw His star in the east and came to worship; the shepherds saw the star, brilliant and breaking up the night, and bowed to worship. When I first heard

Christ called "the morning star" (2 Pet. 1:19), my breath stopped. What a glorious name for the one who ends the night!

But before ending the night, Christ endured the darkness. Nighttime found Him wrestling with His calling alone in the garden. At night He awakened His sleeping disciples, then was abandoned. Darkness brought the religious establishment with their weapons of war to arrest Him. A long night of battering in captivity preceded His journeying through the streets amid jeers and further bloodying in the midst of emotional and spiritual night. Jesus' words to the religious at His arrest broadcast the haunting truth: "This is your hour—when darkness reigns" (Luke 22:53 NIV).

Darkness also symbolizes grief. Just as people wear black to denote mourning, so the three hours of darkness that draped over the earth while Jesus hung from the cross reveal the grief of heaven. The entire earth wore a mantle of bereavement with its King nailed to a tree. For the next two days, darkness and night ruled; but when Christ, the Morning Star, rose from the dead, He abolished forever the curse of darkness. Grief may endure for the night, but joy comes in the morning.

LISTEN

"Who is among you that fears the LORD, that obeys the voice of His servant, that walks in darkness and has no light? Let him trust in the name of the LORD and rely on his God" (Isa. 50:10).

LEARN

And though this world, with devils filled, should
threaten to undo us,
We will not fear, for God hath willed His truth to
triumph through us:
The Prince of Darkness grim, we tremble not for him;
His rage we can endure, for lo, his doom is sure,
One little word shall fell him.

—Martin Luther

So I go on, not knowing,
I would not, if I might.
I would rather walk in the dark with God
Than go alone in the light.
I would rather walk with Him by Faith
Than walk alone by sight.

—Mary Gardner Brainard

LIVE

What effect does darkness have on you? When do you succumb to the night?

How do you stand against the dark, separating the dark from the light?

When do you find joy in the morning? And how?

13

GROANS IN THE GARDEN

The temptation and treason, the violence at night in the garden, result from the bondage of a world traumatized by Eden's events. The earth, cursed because of unfaithfulness, groans in slavery. Earthquakes, sinkholes, droughts, famines, floods, tornadoes, tidal waves, and tsunamis—creation groans as it waits for redemption.

The earth still bears the consequence of our sins. "How long is the land to mourn and the vegetation of the countryside to wither?" Jeremiah asks. "For the wickedness of those who dwell in it, animals and birds have been snatched away, because men have said, 'He will not see our latter ending'" (Jer. 12:4).

Paul picked up on this theme: "For the anxious longing of the creation waits eagerly" (Rom. 8:19). The world eagerly awaits the new heaven and the new earth. Like a restless crowd anxious to view the finished masterpiece, creation groans for the unveiling of the children of God. "And not only this," Paul said, "but also we ourselves, having the first fruits of the Spirit, even we ourselves groan within ourselves, waiting eagerly for our adoption as sons, the redemption of our body" (8:23). Our bodies groan, waiting for full deliverance, as a pregnant woman waits to give birth. We wait, knowing God has good in store for us. These groanings anticipate what God will do in us, through us, and with us as God conforms us fully into the image of the Son.

Our bodies groan too because though our spirits are alive in Christ, our bodies are dying (Rom. 8:10). A neighbor said to me, watching me tear into a tree with a pickax, "I used to be able to do that." I watch our little grandchild, sitting with one leg tucked under her and the other straight out in front, and say, "I don't remember ever being that flexible." Our bodies were compromised in the first garden, and though Christ gives life to our spirits, our "house" continues to be temporary, and flawed. Even as Jesus tabernacled among us, so we tent-camp now, in skin and bones crafted from dust and all too soon returning to dust.

While these earthly confines trap us (2 Cor. 5:2, 5), how much of nipping, tucking, and rearranging is related to a subliminal longing for our new resurrection bodies? Don't we ache to be free from our constant wrong choices and death-doings? Wordless groans express the deepest longings of our hearts, without words to pray and beseech our God. And here we see again God's sensitivity to us, preparation for us, and the desire to emancipate us. God was not deaf to Israel's pleas enslaved in Egypt. "During that long period, the king of Egypt died. The Israelites groaned in their slavery and cried out, and their cry for help because of their slavery went up to God. God heard their groaning and he remembered his covenant with Abraham, with Isaac and with Jacob. So God looked on the Israelites and was concerned about them" (Ex. 2:23–25 NIV).

And just so, God hears our groanings now. The Scriptures comfort us: "The Spirit also helps our weakness; for we do not know how to pray as we should, but the Spirit Himself intercedes for us with groanings too deep for words; and He who searches the hearts knows what the mind of the Spirit is, because He intercedes for the saints according to the will of God" (Rom. 8:26–27).

We are not left groaning and trapped, enslaved in a body with no deliverance. No, though we might be mute, the Spirit speaks for us; though we see no one standing between us, pleading for us, the Spirit interprets our longings before the throne.

One glorious day, all creation will be set free from slavery to corruption into freedom (Rom. 8:21). We saw a foreshadowing of this when Jesus on the cross "cried out again with a loud voice, and yielded up His spirit. And behold, the . . . earth shook; and the rocks were split. The tombs were opened, and many bodies of the saints who had fallen asleep were raised" (Matt. 27:50–52). For a moment, Christ's groan set creation free, and the earth groaned and gave up the dead and acknowledged the Lord of all the universe.

Though we stand too often in darkness, betrayal, and temptation, though we groan before the redemption of the earth and our own redemption as children of God, God sees us, even as God sees Christ the Son. Because the Christ of the garden stands between us and God, and we are indeed complete in Him.

LISTEN

"The joyful anticipation deepens. All around us we observe a pregnant creation. The difficult times of pain throughout the world are simply birth pangs. But it's not only around us; it's within us. The Spirit of God is arousing us within. We're also feeling the birth pangs. These sterile and barren bodies of ours are yearning for full deliverance. That is why waiting does not diminish us, any more than waiting diminishes a pregnant mother. We are enlarged in the waiting. We, of course, don't see what is enlarging us. But the longer we wait, the larger we become, and the more joyful our expectancy. Meanwhile, the moment we get tired in the waiting, God's Spirit is right alongside helping us along. If we don't know how or what to pray, it doesn't matter. He does our praying in and for us, making prayer out of our wordless sighs, our aching groans. He knows us far better than we know ourselves . . . and keeps us present before God. That's why we can be so sure that every detail in our lives of love for God is working into something good" (Rom. 8:21–28 MSG).

LEARN

"Our longing desires can no more exhaust the fullness of the treasures of the Godhead, than our imagination can touch their measure" (MacDonald, *Unspoken*).

"See every little flower straighten its stalk, lift up its neck, and with outstretched head stand expectant: something more than the sun, greater than the light, is coming, is coming—none the less surely coming that it is long upon the road! What matters today, or tomorrow, or ten thousand years to Life himself, to Love himself! He is coming, is coming, and the necks of all humanity are stretched out to see him come!" (MacDonald, *Lilith*).

LIVE

In what ways are you aware of your own deep groanings? When have you experienced the Holy Spirit groaning through you? How are you at hearing the groanings of others, and how do you respond?

Describe your greatest physical pain. Compare that anguish with the longing of creation for relief. What about your longings?

What is it like for you to wait expectantly for God's deliverance of you from groaning and suffering? How do you keep waiting expectantly?

PART 4

SHAME IN THE GARDEN

"I'm ashamed of you!" The mother's eyebrows knitted together, a frown puckering her mouth. Her jaws snapped up and down like a bear trap. "How could you do that?"

"Shame on you!" the father said by his actions, as he redid the chores assigned to his child.

"Shameless!" we say of the brazen woman dressed seductively.

"You should be ashamed of yourself." "Aren't you ashamed of yourself?" "You never get it right." "Only a B? You should get As." "Why aren't you earning more?" "Why didn't you get a different job?"

"Shame on me," we tell ourselves, working harder, or avoiding relationships, or losing ourselves in compulsive behavior.

Whether conveyed through words, tone, attitude, or posture, shame happens. It happens when we don't measure up, don't do something perfectly, and feel another's censure for our failure. We interpret it as a global personality problem, a defect in our being, and come to the conclusion not that we *made* a mistake, but that we *are* a mistake.

Shame entered the human race when Adam and Eve, having eaten the only expressly forbidden fruit in the entire garden, covered themselves and hid from God. But throughout the Scriptures, we find people who should be covered with shame but are not because they have recovered the freedom lost in Eden—freedom found only in the wholehearted embrace of God. "Those who looked to him were radiant; their faces are never covered with shame" (Ps. 34:5 NIV). In our journey from Eden to Gethsemane, we trace the trail of shame and look to Christ, who endured the cross, despising its shame, and learn new strategies for shameless living.

14

SHAME IN EDEN

How does shame fit into this cozy garden scenario? It doesn't. We can't imagine a more perfect setting, nor can we grasp the freedom Adam and Eve experienced in Eden. Though it lingers just outside the edges of our dreams, and we sense this perfection nearby, it evades us. Fresh-faced with wonder, they romped, tasted, and enjoyed the very best life God could provide for them. The most exotic and elaborate garden in our world today wilts in comparison with Eden; it's a wonder Adam and Eve's hearts didn't burst from the fullness of joy. And I have to ask, what was it like in a garden without mosquitoes? Adam and Eve had no worries in this area, or they wouldn't have walked around in the buff. The Scriptures recount in modest form their early experience in Eden: "And the man and his wife were both naked and were not ashamed" (Gen. 2:25).

Unless the Scriptures employ time-lapse techniques here, the clock has not moved forward much between their shame-free living and the serpent's approach. The very next verse in Scripture hisses at us: "Now the serpent was more crafty than any beast of the field which the LORD God had made. And he said to the woman . . ." (Gen. 3:1). Warning drums sound in our head, like the ominous music from *Jaws*, pushing us to the edge of our seat and elevating our heart rate. "Watch out! Trouble ahead! Snake crossing!" Because we know this scene. We've watched the movie, read the book, have the lines memorized.

Spoiler alert: The scene we are about to watch is the first recorded incidence of shame.

Shame, as we now know it, stands separate from the traditional dictionary definition of guilt. Humiliation, wanting to cringe into a tiny, invisible ball and self-destruct, is closer to the current meaning. Shame, according to Ronald and Patricia Potter-Efron, is "a painful belief in one's basic defectiveness as a human being." Even knowing in our brains that God loves us doesn't always automatically eliminate our base of shame. Shame exists both within and without the body of Christ and is a learned response to the messages of those around us.

There is something amazing and astounding about Adam and Eve's ability to be naked and unashamed. I will never forget one of our small children standing on the bathroom counter, stark naked after a bath, smiling at the mirror image. Smiling. No one does that after the age of, say, five. Body shame traces back through the centuries like a slug leaving a tacky trail. I've heard stories of women bathing in the privacy of their own bathroom with a gown covering them, coached not to look at themselves naked or even in a mirror because the body was something to be avoided, a tool easily accessed by sin. The body is evil; don't look.

Horror stories return like nightmares from junior-high gym class and the locker room, where the gym teacher stood at the shower door with a clipboard and class roster, placing a dark pencil check mark next to our name as we entered the shower. At least in the girls' locker room, the community shower was enough to cause death by mortification; better to be graded down and avoid the embarrassment of body comparison. The hideous Popeye gym suits of my childhood should have been sufficient for keeping students humble; the mandatory shower, however, struck students in their area of greatest embarrassment.

Most people who survive life past toddlerhood are uncomfortable with nakedness—their own or another's. In the original garden, then, it makes sense that Satan would slither into the picture at precisely the time Adam and Eve were unashamed of their nakedness. We have been embarrassed about our bodies ever since.

We become vulnerable when we love others, opening ourselves up to the possibility of shame. We become vulnerable, naked, when we attempt new things, risk attaining a dream, try to tell another the truth in love. We become vulnerable when we ask for forgiveness, confessing to a darkness within or a failing. When we are vulnerable, we are easy game for the predator, shame.

Ironically, we also display our shame base when we make ourselves overly visible. It is possible, I think, that shame shows up both in embarrassment over our bodies *and*, in a perverse way, in a flaunting of our bodies. So what some would call shameless behavior is actually a fighting against the voice of shame. The desperate near-nudity in our culture is actually revealing the essence of shame, which is separation from our identity in Christ.

While it looks like the opposite of the "Don't look at me; I'm naked" shame, it is really another side of the same leaf, an attempt to appear acceptable on someone else's terms. Either extreme reveals our brokenness and separation from God.

Working on the area of doubt, Satan is also a pro. He slithered up to Eve when she was vulnerable, unashamed, and then moved to a chink in her invisible armor: "You sure God said that, honey? No, surely He didn't say that!" At his words, Eve doubted both her memory and God's goodness. Doubt is a great shame inducer, making us wonder if something is wrong with us, with our memories. Whether we doubt ourselves, our God-given abilities, or God, we give Satan a free slide into the garden.

The serpent loves to inspire doubt and twist the truth. With just his slight shifting of the words, Eve was hooked. "Indeed, has God said, 'You shall not eat from *any* tree of the garden'?" (Gen. 3:1, emphasis added). Shame tends to believe the other is always right and we are always wrong, or vice versa.

To wriggle away from the garden piranha, Eve could have refused to argue. This is a super strategy for parents, for people in conflict, for us. Don't get lured into an argument or debate about a third party. Instead, send the doubter to the original source. "Talk to God about that, Satan. God will set you straight." But we love to argue, and Eve somehow felt compelled to enter into a dialogue with this beautiful and clever companion. Unfortunately, she chose to elaborate on God's original prohibition, which put her right into the Enemy's clutches. Self-doubt, and the need to defend herself, kicked in, and she put words in God's mouth: "You shall not eat from it or touch it, or you will die" (Gen. 3:3). Touch wasn't prohibited; eating was.

Satan, the consummate deceiver, sows a little more doubt for good measure: "You surely will not die!" (3:4). Eve believed his bold lie, and Adam believed Eve; they both ended up separated from their true identity in God and hid when they heard God's footsteps in the garden.

Hiding when we feel shame is a common response. When we're snared in a trap, found to be wrong, or are just being fresh-faced and honest, we easily embrace shame from others and from our own internal shame monitor. We hide when we remove ourselves from relationships, when we clam up, turn away, cold shoulder, and blame others.

God's response to Adam and Eve touches me. Yes, there is a consequence to their sin, but God's immediate answer to their hiding and their shame is one of love and sacrifice. God's sorrow and heartbreak over their choices and their loss of innocence are woven between the lines as our God tenderly covers their nakedness with fur.

Still, we find ourselves, with them, cast out from Eden, stumbling around in shame, unable to accept the covering, unable to embrace the truth—that God loved us from the beginning and would rather die than have us separated from Him.

LISTEN

"Fear not, for you will not be put to shame; and do not feel humiliated, for you will not be disgraced; but you will forget the shame of your youth, and the reproach of your widowhood you will remember no more. For your husband is your Maker, whose name is the LORD of hosts; and your Redeemer is the Holy One of Israel, who is called the God of all the earth" (Isa. 54:4–5).

LEARN

"Shame entered the human drama as a result of sin. Broken fellowship with God meant broken fellowship with each other. Separation from God caused an internal separation and a relational separation. Adam and Eve were no longer true to their soulful selves, nor were they true to one another. 'Shame is the expression of the fact that we no longer accept the other person as the gift of God,' writes Dietrich Bonhoeffer. 'In the unity of unbroken obedience man is naked in the presence of man, uncovered, revealing both body and soul, and yet he is not ashamed. Shame only comes into existence in the world of division.' The root cause of shame is the unnatural, disobedient and dysfunctional violation of body and soul. Sin makes us terribly vulnerable, insecure and fundamentally dissatisfied with ourselves and others" (Webster).

LIVE

When are you most susceptible to shame? What incidents of you shaming others do you recall?

Where do you hear shaming messages and from whom? In what setting? How often is your shame reaction based on old messages rather than current messages?

What message do you hear from God regarding shame? How do you turn away from shame and toward God and relationships with others?

15

SHAME BETWEEN THE GARDENS

In a world that determines acceptability with a tape measure, IQ test, or bank statement, shame becomes a natural companion. Everywhere we turn, status symbols remind us of our failure to excel, our falling short of perfection. Tim felt ashamed and emasculated because, in spite of a master's degree, his pay as a minister prohibited him from buying a home for his family or driving a decent car. For Pete, shame hid behind bravado, in boasting and bragging about accomplishments and popularity. If he could only elevate himself in the world's eyes, perhaps he could lose his high level of shame, of chronic not-enoughness.

Whether we compare bust size or running times, offspring or investments, we cannot win this game. The cards always stack against us when we internalize the message that we are failures if we don't look, act, or speak a certain way. If extreme, chronic shame hisses in our ear, "You're a mistake. You should never have been born." When we look to others for approval or identity, we set up camp in uninhabitable land, exiled from Eden but prohibited from entering into the benefits of Gethsemane.

We drag shame about our own inadequacies, failings, and mistakes. Shame shows up when we connect another's actions or reputation to our own sense of worth. After ten years, Lucille finally recognized that she'd hauled shame around with her like a truckload of compost ever since her daughter's divorce. She believed that divorce simply shouldn't happen in a Christian family, and her daughter's failed marriage meant that Lucille failed to raise her properly.

We carry shame over our pasts. Imperfect parents unintentionally heap shame upon us. Incorporating failures and mistakes into our personality, never relinquishing them to God, can increase our shame. Pain from childhood—living with abuse, alcoholism or other addiction, neglect, abandonment, lies, poverty—settles like clay into the bottom of our hearts, stopping us from drinking in the love of God, letting shame seep through our souls until we feel shame over issues and problems we didn't cause. Shame because we're different, because our homes were or are unsafe, because everyone else on earth but us lived a "normal" life. We lug shame from the past into our families and pass down shame to the next generation when we continue to hide from the pain instead of dealing with the pain. Many families have subjects no one is allowed to discuss, and these are guns loaded with shame.

Shame grows in the presence of constant correction; we add to shame with our own compulsions and behaviors. Shame rears its head in our homes, churches, communities, and workplaces when we never allow or acknowledge ourselves to be wrong.

This parasite preys on our souls, sucking the life from our relationships. It keeps us from trusting others, from developing close friendships, from real vulnerability. Shame also hinders us from experiencing real forgiveness in Christ.

Though we might not call it a disease, symptoms alert us to the presence of shame. Watch for labels—people labeling us or our labeling others. "You're an idiot!" "What a loser." Name-calling in general can increase shame. One young mother introduced her rambunctious toddler as "my little monster" until she realized that such a name labeled him and might cause him to grow into exactly that. Calling people, including ourselves, only names that edify is a discipline important to cultivate. Statements like, "I'm ashamed of you" and "You should be ashamed of yourself" cannot be helpful either. Other statements to avoid include, "How dare you!" and "How could you?"

Here are additional signs that shame lurks like a snake—and not a harmless garden snake—in the weeds, waiting to overcome us. Symptoms of shame include: anger, boasting, blaming, perfectionism, defensiveness, edginess, fatigue, underachieving, and poor self-care.

Shame helps us when it flags our attention. Look at others' messages and your own internal whisperings: "You don't measure up. You're a failure. A mistake. Worthless. Your body is inadequate, defective, below average." Hear what the shoulds say: "You should earn more money so you can prove yourself worthy. You should keep a cleaner house, be unfailingly kind and polite, cross off everything on the to-do list. You should drive a better car, have children who are model citizens, and earn your parents' approval. You should have unlimited funds, be able to function without sleep, and smile at all times. You should never be upset, angry, or anything but happy."

These are the whisperings of shame, the voice of the serpent, who ever seeks to separate us from the love of God, the adequacy of Christ, and the perfection of His covering.

But shame also shows us where we can grow, where we need to laugh, where we are safe or unsafe in relationships. Tim, for instance, ashamed because of his inability to provide better for his family, picked up on the shame, turning it into a tool for growth. He determined to use his financial state as a time to learn humility, to identify with the poorer people in his community, and to teach himself and his children to detach their self-worth from their possessions. We believe the saying, "What doesn't kill you makes you stronger." So we listen to the niggling voice because it teaches us where we can trust God more, where we can learn anew to rely on Christ's accomplishment on our behalf.

We listen, and we look to Gethsemane for Christ's strategy in handling shame.

LISTEN

"The LORD your God is in your midst, a victorious warrior. He will exult over you with joy, He will be quiet in His love, He will rejoice over you with shouts of joy. . . . Behold, I am going to deal at that time with all your oppressors, I will save the lame and gather the outcast, and I will turn their shame into praise and renown in all the earth" (Zeph. 3:17, 19).

LEARN

Notoriously, many addictions are characterized by shame. "People become addicted to a substance or to an activity as a way of dealing with or covering up their shame." Time and time again he has seen how an addict "carries an enormous—although often secret—burden of shame. For that reason, whenever shame is present addiction is predictable" (Hemfelt, Minerth, Meier).

LIVE

What symptoms of shame do you notice in your own life? In the lives of people you love?

What primary shaming messages do you hear? Where do you think your shame primarily originates?

When has shame become a tool for growth? How?

16

SHAME IN THE SECOND GARDEN

Hebrews 12:2 says, "Fixing our eyes on Jesus, the author and perfecter of faith, who for the joy set before Him endured the cross, *despising the shame*, and has sat down at the right hand of the throne of God" (emphasis added). Christ understood shame more deeply than we will ever experience—shame in relationship to the cross and to His true identity.

Jesus knew the Scripture, "If someone guilty of a capital offense is put to death and their body is exposed on a pole, you must not leave the body hanging on the pole overnight. Be sure to bury it that same day, because anyone who is hung on a pole is under God's curse" (Deut. 21:22–23 NIV; see also Gal. 3:13). Typically in Old Testament times, hanging wasn't a means of death, but a sequel to death. Hanging on a crude wooden beam, post, or tree "exposed the corpse to ultimate disgrace," according to Charles Ryrie in his footnote on Deuteronomy 21:23. Christ knew this, but somehow "despised the shame" of the cross. The ultimate shame of the cross was that it labeled Christ as a sinner separated from God.

Here, the word for *shame* comes from a term meaning disfigurement. Not only was the cross physically disfiguring, but shame leads us to see ourselves as deformed and hideous. Shame also has its roots in a word for "dishonest," and this is the ultimate dishonesty: the holy Son of God charged as a criminal and hung on a cross to die. Yet He gladly took the disfiguring label of criminal, of sinner, for our sakes that we might never again be separated from Him.

In our own world, shame is also dishonesty; shame lies to us, telling us we are defective, problematic, and a mistake. But Christ stands against this lie with His life, His death, and His promise to love us. Look at Hebrews 2:11: Christ isn't *ashamed* to call us His family. In fact, the prospect of fulfilling God's calling of Him and of bringing us into His family filled Him with joy—"the joy set before Him" (12:2)—and allowed Him to endure the cross and despise its shame. Christ knew who He was and refused to allow shame to disfigure Him or dissuade Him from His purpose.

If we fix our eyes on Jesus, we begin to understand who we are, as well, and learn to despise the shame.

LISTEN

"Those who look to him are radiant; their faces are never covered with shame" (Ps. 34:5 NIV).

LEARN

Shame feelings should lead us to God, who never covers us with shame, but instead covers us with Jesus Christ. Put on Christ. Cover yourself with Christ, the Christ who endured the cross but stood against the disfigurement of the cross's reputation. Shame can lead us to dishonesty, a covering up of truth. See what Adam and Eve did immediately upon realizing how suddenly far they were from their ideal, their creation in God's image? Shame defaces us so we no longer know our own value and who we are. But when we realize that we are the beloved, our shame level drops. Why? Because we learn in the presence of Christ that "there is now no condemnation for those who are in Christ Jesus" (Rom. 8:1).

LIVE

How does Christ's enduring the cross, despising the shame, impact you?

How often is shame a factor that keeps you from Christ? From others?

How do you think Christ feels about you, your shame, your soul? What changes for you when you think about the possibility that you are part of the joy set before Him?

17

SHAMELESS STRATEGIES

How do we stand against feelings of shame? The word for *despise* in Hebrews 12:2 means just that. Christ strongly opposed or stood against the shame of the cross. Following are some strategies that help us not be disfigured by shame, but to look to Him and become radiant.

Stand in grace. In 2 Samuel 22:17–20, God rescued David because God delighted in him. Listen to the voice of God delighting in you—for is that not the truth?—and let God rescue you from shame.

Rejoice in hope. When we, in hope, cling to Christ tenaciously as climbing ivy we will never be disappointed (see Rom. 5:1–5).

Refuse to listen. Eve didn't turn her back on the serpent, but we can once we recognize his voice.

Examine and dispel the shame. Look for truth hidden in the curse. For instance, if you often come away from an interaction with someone feeling a sense of shame, something about that relationship isn't safe, what can be done to create safety with that person?

Exchange the lies for truth. "I am fearfully and wonderfully made; wonderful are Your works, and my soul knows it very well" (Ps. 139:14). Yes, sin misshapes and disfigures us, but God forgives and restores.

Look to God. "In you, LORD, I have taken refuge; let me never be put to shame" (Ps. 71:1 NIV).

Know the inheritance. "Instead of your shame you will receive a double portion, and instead of disgrace you will rejoice in your inheritance" (Isa. 61:7 NIV). Shame is no longer our lot, no longer our inheritance from the fall in Eden.

LISTEN

"The LORD your God . . . has worked wonders for you; never again will my people be shamed. Then you will know that I am in Israel, that I am the LORD your God, and that there is no other; never again will my people be shamed" (Joel 2:26–27 NIV).

LEARN

When we are set free from shame, an interesting phenomenon happens in community. When we can be real before God, we ultimately find acceptance and love. We're free to be wrong, to be vulnerable; we no longer have to be perfect. Church then becomes a safe place and refuge for others. They are drawn in. How amazing that Christ turns our shame and failure into a tool for reaching others! Yet again, Christ has the final say in the battle with the serpent.

LIVE

How do you resist shame? What tools can you employ to stand against its deforming power?

What relationships seem to perpetuate your shame? What can you do in those places?

How do you give grace, embrace others in the loving acceptance of God, and resist the temptation to shame another?

PART 5

SACRIFICE IN THE GARDEN

Crammed into a small plane seat as a fresh-from-college graduate, I pored over the opening chapters of the Bible, reading and underlining and then stopping to cry. Christ's sacrifice was foretold in the garden of Eden! From the very beginning, the Trinity made plans to redeem human beings from their fallen state. What amazing love—this just-made world, crafted so beautifully and with such tenderness for us, and so quickly brought to bear the curse of our fallenness. Even then, Christ planned to give up heaven, come to earth, and offer up the final sacrifice for our sin. My soul stumbles over this truth, stumbled then as a young adult and stumbles now as a young adult.

I recognized my own patterns in Adam and Eve's cover-up for sin, the first pathetic human attempt at looking good in another's sight—and God's. Tracing the sacrifices from Eden through the Old Testament, learning that they ended with Christ at Gethsemane, moved and wooed me and nestled into the layers of my mind and heart. God's sacrificial love pours over the Scriptures and zooms through history all the way to my own life and brings me to my knees in worship.

18

SACRIFICE IN EDEN

Adam and Eve's story is about selfishness, grasping for control, glory, and godlike power. But sacrifice is also part of the scene. They sacrificed—gave up, relinquished, exchanged—the life in Eden for something that looked better. Suddenly, they were tarnished, jaded, and self-serving, and their idea of a covering for their sin was more a cover-up: ripping leaves off fig trees in a dying tear in order to hide. Most sobering, they sacrificed their relationship with God, allowing the world and all its temptations to come between them, to usurp God's place in their souls and lives. In Eden began the reign of self, and to this day it is our greatest temptation, and perhaps the root of our sinful acts.

Adam and Eve's idea of atonement—of covering for their sin—was deficient; cold, bloodless leaves couldn't reestablish their relationship with God or cleanse them from the ugliness of their sin. Their inadequate and imperfect sacrifice glared in light of God's next move, God's sacrifice.

A sacrifice, to be a real sacrifice, cannot be self-serving; God sacrificed with forethought and thoroughness, assuring that their covering was competent, the sacrifice sufficient.

Even with the damaging and hurtful betrayal by these treasured children, God's forgiving, redemptive love enfolded them. "The LORD God made garments of skin for Adam and his wife, and clothed them" (Gen. 3:21). Not until later do we learn that "without shedding of blood there is no forgiveness" (Heb. 9:22). But God, in grace, foreshadowed the coming sacrificial system and the ultimate sacrifice of the Son when He killed the animals and covered Adam and Eve, not with leaves, but with fur from the first of creation.

God's sacrifices go deeper than skinning a couple of animals, however. God sacrificed—gave up, relinquished, exchanged—the desire and right for first place in our lives. God wanted—and still wants—to be the perfect lover, the all-consuming passion, of this creation but gave up the right to control us. This lover allowed Adam and Eve, and allows us, to choose to love in response.

God also in the garden so long ago gave up dreams for our very best—the perfect life—and gave us the choice of returning on our own to relationship with our creator. And then, in an act of great compassion, He relinquished judgment, exchanging it for mercy, and presented us with the option of coming home.

Did God's heart bleed, sacrificing the animals in the garden? God's parent-heart longed for His children, for their wholeness, for their love. So God exchanged the life of the animals for the lives of Adam and Eve.

LISTEN

"Surely the arm of the LORD is not too short to save, nor his ear too dull to hear. But your iniquities have separated you from your God; your sins have hidden his face from you, so that he will not hear. . . . The LORD looked and was displeased that there was no justice. He saw that there was no one, he was appalled that there was no one to intervene; so his own arm achieved salvation for him, and his own righteousness sustained him" (Isa. 59:1–2, 15–16 NIV).

LEARN

I stand amazed in the presence
Of Jesus the Nazarene,
And wonder how He could love me,
A sinner, condemned, unclean.

For me it was in the garden
He prayed: "Not My will, but Thine."
He had no tears for His own griefs,
But sweat drops of blood for mine.

In pity angels beheld Him,
And came from the world of light
To comfort Him in the sorrows
He bore for my soul that night.

He took my sins and my sorrows,
He made them His very own;
He bore the burden to Calvary,
And suffered and died alone.

When with the ransomed in glory
His face I at last shall see,
'Twill be my joy through the ages
To sing of His love for me.

—Charles Gabriel

LIVE

When has an action of yours caused another to sacrifice? What was that like for you?

How do you cover over your sins, mistakes, and failures?

What has God done to bring you back?

19

THE SACRIFICIAL SYSTEM

Following the eviction from Eden, the famous first offspring, Cain and Abel, offered their own sacrifices: one veggies, another meat. Rather than examining whether the offering itself was deficient or God was really picky, we look at the heart of the one offering the sacrifice. Competition, covetousness, and a selfish interest in his own well-being filled Cain's heart. "What? You think I'm gonna look after my brother?" Perhaps nothing at all was wrong with the offering of "fruits of the soil" (Gen. 4:3) that Cain sacrificed to God. Darkness, however, filled him, and God saw it.

Sacrifice has more to do with the state of our heart than the value of the offering itself. Sacrifices demonstrate not our wealth, but the depth of our love. Still, in a world where the visible is valued and the bigger the better (house, car, salary, muscle, etc.), we easily pervert the idea of sacrifice. If it makes us look good or somehow covers up our failings, we go for it, long for it, buy it, offer it, and clang cymbals along the way to make sure it's noticed.

Just prior to exiting Egypt, the Israelites ate a Passover dinner, including bread without leaven (leaven being a symbol for sin) and a perfect lamb without spot or blemish, whose blood covered the doorframes and signaled that the angel of death would pass over those dwelling within. That covering of blood saved the Israelites from death.

Throughout the Old Testament, after God instituted the sacrificial system, a complex system of various offerings designed to help us move back into relationship with God, we hear refrains of "I desire obedience and not sacrifice." Why? Because a sacrifice is a giving back, an offering of joy, thanksgiving, repentance, sorrow, and fellowship. The word *offering* has as its root meaning "to draw near," and our offerings, our sacrifices, should be just that—given out of a loving desire to draw near to God. But the Israelites turned this gracious opportunity to love God and restore their relationship with Him into an ugly attempt to buy His favor to secure social standing and political correctness. Maybe, like the Israelites, we use sacrifices as a magic remedy, a "Sunday-morning-after" solution to a week—or a life— of wantonness and idolatry. Yes, of course God wants obedience that flows out of love.

We, too, use the system. Our attempts at sacrifice, like the Israelites', are wretchedly incomplete, covered with the soot of impure motives, and corrupted by vanity.

Perhaps we unintentionally sacrifice our families, marriages, friends, gifts, and dreams to all-consuming jobs, debts, or even hobbies. Or we view the "system" of religious rightness as a balance scale, where this "sacrifice" (time, money, attendance at church, charitable work, committees) is an atonement, a means of covering up our failures to meet God's standards. We live in constant motion to avoid facing the truth: None of our sacrifices make us whole.

Just as Adam and Eve's sacrifice—their leaf covering, their atonement—would wither and fall off, so do our sacrifices, our attempts to buy merit and cover up our deficiencies and failings. They shrivel and crumble and eventually reveal that which we wanted so desperately to camouflage: our failings and our sins that ever separate us from God. We can't clothe ourselves with good works; in the bright light of God's holiness, they're filthy rags. We cannot complete ourselves. We can only be complete and completely covered with the sacrifice of One, the perfect sacrifice that clothes, cleanses, and completes us.

All our works, then, are to proceed as gifts from us to God for the glory of God. They are never to be attempts at looking good, though frequently the Holy Spirit reminds me that I seek too often my own glory and not God's, or that my desires are split between the two.

Once this week, as fear and weariness again filled my bones with lead and my spirit with clouds, I wondered if my state of constant depletion glorifies God. Does it appeal to God, like some offering or sacrifice, a fragrant aroma? I doubt it. Fear and fatigue don't make God look good. We consider these as altruistic; America and the church institution applauds hard work and its resultant exhaustion. These become, or seem to become, a great sacrifice. But really, they call into question whether God truly is all-powerful, all-knowing, and all-present if I find it necessary to work endlessly, snapping at everyone because my control frays to the last thread and fear gnaws even that strand.

So what I consider sacrificial living is actually self-centered. It harms me, my family, and my relationship with God. A real sacrifice puts the focus on God. And this leads us to the ultimate, final, and only true sacrifice for our sins. It leads us to the garden, to Gethsemane, Golgotha, and the empty tomb.

LISTEN

"This is how much God loved the world: He gave his Son, his one and only Son. And this is why: so that no one need be destroyed; by believing in him, anyone can have a whole and lasting life. God didn't go to all the trouble of sending his Son merely to point an accusing finger, telling the world how bad it was. He came to help, to put the world right again. Anyone who trusts in him is acquitted; anyone who refuses to trust him has long

since been under the death sentence without knowing it"
(John 3:16–18 MSG).

LEARN

"When Christ calls a man, he bids him come and die"
(Bonhoeffer, *Cost*).

LIVE

What superficial sacrifices have you offered?

How are they self-centered?

What's at the root of such a sacrifice (for example,
fear, perfectionism, workaholism, self-righteousness,
etc.)? Can you excavate those roots with the God of all
mercy?

20

THE FINAL SACRIFICE

What can be said about Christ's sacrifice without trivializing it? The most profound and complete work ever done on behalf of a human being, since God created us in the image of the triune God, was done by Christ. Theologians spend their entire lives thinking about the sacrifice of Jesus Christ. A quick search by subject reveals thousands and thousands of books about Jesus. How can these few pages cover the depth and breadth of such an enormous, mysterious, and profound topic?

Can we even begin to grasp what it means for the almighty God to leave heaven and come to earth? And as a baby no less? And then the baby grows up into a man who is still God but lays aside His God-hood and lives just like we do, only perfectly, and then dies for us. And this man, who presents himself as a sacrifice for us, fulfills the entire sacrificial system set up in the Old Testament, a system based on farm animals and agriculture, a system begun in a world still fresh from creation.

No one has ever done anything like this in all of human history. It's so far beyond my fragile ability to form words and sentences; it fills me so full that I can't think. In fact, even as I dwell on these facts, this immense love of God, of Jesus Christ, for me overwhelms me. No one has ever loved me like this before. No one can ever love you like this, except for God.

Christ's sacrifice began in Eden, as He prepared even then to come in the flesh, to live life shaped like us, that we might be restored to the image of God. Christ sacrificed His place in heaven, gave up all the rights of His deity, and "emptied Himself." By "being found in appearance as a man" (Phil. 2:7–8), Christ did what we could never do for ourselves. Assuming human flesh, He set about living the life God had designed for us, a life of total reliance on God. Adam and Eve wouldn't, then couldn't, live in this way, so Christ took our frame and lived it for us in our place. Though tempted in all ways as humans are, He remained sinless, perfect. He not only comes to our aid when we are tempted, but He fulfilled all the demands of the perfection-seeking law.

Just look at the sacrifices in the Old Testament (see Lev. 1–6; 23). Christ fulfilled every single one of them.

The burnt offering: This offering was a voluntary act of worship, an atonement for unintentional sin in general, an expression of devotion, commitment, and complete surrender to God. In Gethsemane, Jesus said, "Not My will, but Yours be done" (Luke 22:42).

The grain offering: "I am the bread of life" (John 6:35).

The peace offering: "He Himself is our peace" (Eph. 2:14).

The sin offering and the trespass offering: Both were fulfilled by the perfect, sinless life of Christ. "He committed no sin, and no deceit was found in his mouth. . . . 'He himself bore our sins' in his body on the cross, so that we might die to sins and live for righteousness; 'by his wounds you have been healed'" (1 Pet. 2:22, 24 NIV; see also Isa. 53:10).

The drink offering: "Let anyone who is thirsty come to me and drink" (John 7:37 NIV). "Whoever drinks the water that I give them will never thirst. Indeed, the water I give them will become in them a spring of water welling up to eternal life" (John 4:14 NIV). "He poured out Himself to death" (Isa. 53:12).

And don't forget the timing: Christ was crucified at the exact moment of the morning sacrifice in the temple, and He died at the precise time of the evening sacrifice. And the Passover supper? Christ became that perfect Lamb, without spot or blemish. "Behold, the Lamb of God who takes away the sin of the world!" (John 1:29).

We could continue with the feasts in Scripture, and marvel at how Christ's crucifixion, death, and resurrection coincide with all the feasts except the Feast of

Trumpets. (He is saving that for the last, when the Lord returns with a blast of trumpets!) We could look at Abraham's covenant with God, when God agreed to keep heaven's part of the bargain and human beings would keep theirs; and how God not only kept heaven's side, but sent the Son to keep the human side.

We can look at all these remarkable examples of Christ's fulfillment by His own sacrifice. And surely, after all this, our hearts are moved by His love for us, we are on the floor bowed in worship, sacrifices of praise and thanksgiving flow from our lips.

We can add nothing to the sacrifice. There no longer remains any sacrifice for our sin. With the shedding of Christ's blood, His sinless life became the only possible atonement for sin. Jesus the Messiah did what we cannot do. And now He stands between us and God, ever covering us with himself, the perfect covering, the perfect clothing, the perfect sacrifice.

LISTEN

"First [Christ] said, 'Sacrifices and offerings, burnt offerings and sin offerings you did not desire, nor were you pleased with them' — though they were offered in accordance with the law. Then he said, 'Here I am, I have come to do your will.' He sets aside the first to establish the second. And by that will, we have been made holy through the sacrifice of the body of Jesus

Christ once for all. Day after day every priest stands and performs his religious duties; again and again he offers the same sacrifices, which can never take away sins. But when this priest had offered for all time one sacrifice for sins, he sat down at the right hand of God, and since that time he waits for his enemies to be made his footstool. For by one sacrifice he has made perfect forever those who are being made holy" (Heb. 10:8–14 NIV).

LEARN

"We offer the world and ourselves to God. But we do it in Christ and in remembrance of Him. We do it in Christ because He has already offered all that is to be offered to God. . . . In Him was Life—and this Life of all of us, He gave to God. . . . And we do it in remembrance of Him because, as we offer again and again our life and our world to God, we discover each time that there is nothing else to be offered but Christ Himself—the Life of the world, the fullness of all that exists. . . . We come again and again with our lives to offer; we bring and 'sacrifice'—that is, give to God—what He has given us; and each time we come to the End of all sacrifices, of all offerings . . . because each time it is revealed to us that Christ has offered all that exists, and that He and all that exists has been offered in His offering of Himself" (Schmemann).

LIVE

When did you first become aware that you could never measure up to God's standard? That you needed something to take away your failings? Your sin?

How does it feel to need a sacrifice and to know what Christ did for you, personally? Where are you still trying to make it on your own?

Take time, in silence, to meditate on Christ's sacrifice for you.

21

OUR SACRIFICES TODAY

Christ's death and resurrection abolished the sacrificial system instituted in the garden of Eden and fleshed out in the Old Testament. Sacrifices cannot save us any longer; there no longer remains any sacrifice for our sin. What remains, then, for us? Are the sacrifices over?

The hymn "My Hope Is Built" trumpets the words, "Dressed in His righteousness alone, faultless to stand before the throne." Phrases such as these adorn the New Testament: "put on Christ," "clothe yourselves with Christ." Reminiscent of Adam and Eve when they "put on" leaves—of God when clothing them with warm fur—we can't buy, sell, bleed, work, or atone for our faults and failings; we can't frost them with good deeds and pious living. Christ once and for all completed our need for covering.

Sacrifice implies an exchange, and it's no sacrifice unless we value what we give up. "I don't care; I didn't like it anyway," a teenager says about what seemed a generous giving away of an expensive article of clothing.

Where there's no cost or value to the giver, there's no sacrifice.

The widow, with her gnarled hands and ancient face and timeless faith, sacrificed everything when she put her "mite" in the offering. In an age when women were not supposed to work, a widow was entirely at society's mercy. She had no means of support unless her family provided for her.

Did she waver with her fingertips over the slot in the box? Did she wrestle with her need for money and security, however minuscule that money might be, and her love for God? What happened inside her when she pinched the two pitiful coins between her work-worn fingertips, and then relinquished them?

And to drop them into the offering spout at the temple. This required true faith on her part. Mark's story really begins in 12:38: Jesus warned His followers about the religious elite. "Beware of the scribes . . . who devour widows' houses, and for appearance's sake offer long prayers; these will receive greater condemnation" (12:38, 40). Then Christ sat down opposite the treasury, watched, and redefined sacrifice with the widow's story. Her sacrifice was all the more heartfelt and real because she knew that the religious bureaucrats "devoured widows' houses." Still, she gave all she had—the ultimate sacrifice. How could she offer this sacrifice in light of the flagrant injustice and hypocrisy, knowing that the scribes would never follow the scriptural command to care for widows? Because she saw beyond their posturing and impostering to the core, to the God whose love never left her, even when her husband died, even when the only things between her and absolute destitution were two tiny circles of copper, worth less than a penny.

Paul wrote in Philippians 3:7–9: "But whatever things were gain to me, those things I have counted as loss for the sake of Christ. More than that, I count all things to be loss in view of the surpassing value of know-ing Christ Jesus my Lord, for whom I have suffered the loss of all things, and count them but rubbish so that I may gain Christ, and may be found in Him, not having a righteousness of my own derived from the Law, but that which is through faith in Christ, the righteousness which comes from God on the basis of faith."

With any sacrifice, we face a relinquishment moment: when we hold up the costs of an act or an item, and then give it up. In sacrifice, not only must something be given in exchange for something else, there is that moment of weigh-in when we acknowledge the value of our sacrifice. How dearly do we hold this? What is this worth to me?

And then we die to it. We offer it on the altar in order for something else to grow or come to life or fruition or realization. Sacrifice, seen in this way, is not unlike forgiveness, being willing to bear the cost, pay the price. Archbishop Fulton J. Sheen writes, "Love is capable of overruling, in some way, your natural feelings about pain; that some things which otherwise might be painful are a joy to you when you find they benefit others. . . . Love is the only force in the world which can make pain bearable, and it makes it more than bearable by transforming it into the joy of sacrifice. . . . The deeper our love, the less the sense of pain, and the keener our joy of sacrifice."

It isn't that we don't gain when we sacrifice; our gain isn't the point of the sacrifice (then it's not a sacrifice). We do gain, in fact. We gain the amazing knowledge that God is well-pleased with us, that we have been obedient to God's call on our lives for that moment, that our offering becomes a fragrant aroma to God and to the world, and that we aren't possessed by our possessions. And sacrifice leads to praise, thanksgiving, and joy in the presence of God.

Whether or not another ever sees our giving, comments on it, or benefits from it, God sees. God knows the cost involved, knows our hearts, and swoops in to fill us even more. When we give sacrificially, we become more and more like Christ.

When we search the Scriptures, it turns out that our sacrifices today, though they don't secure the state of our soul, bring God glory. They begin with and in the heart: "For you do not delight in sacrifice, otherwise I would give it; You are not pleased with burnt offering. The sacrifices of God are a broken spirit; a broken and a contrite heart, O God, You will not despise" (Ps. 51:16–17). Other sacrifices for us today are as follows.

"Present your bodies a living and holy sacrifice" (Rom. 12:1). Giving up my life, presenting my body as a living sacrifice, means giving all of myself into God's hands and letting God put me in the right place at the right time. Choosing to listen, grow, and give up becomes a love offering to God.

"Sacrifice of praise" (Heb. 13:15; see also Jer. 17:26). Our sacrifices consist of praise, of lifting up our hands, and a relinquishment. "May the lifting up of my hands be like the evening sacrifice" (Ps. 141:2 NIV).

Sacrifice of obedience (see 1 Sam. 15:22). God no longer delights in burnt offerings and sacrifices; God delights in our obedience. We show our love by the way we live.

"Sacrifice of thanksgiving" (Ps. 116:17; 107:22). How is thanksgiving a sacrifice? It pulls our gaze away from our own sufficiency and concerns, changes our hearts, and refocuses us on God. It's hard to be selfish and thankful at the same time!

Sacrifices of joy, righteousness, doing good and sharing—these sacrifices please God. God desires a broken and contrite heart, a heart that is broken and then filled with love that overflows in a lifestyle of love, mercy, and justice. God doesn't want cold-blooded killing on an altar. God wants a relationship with us, one that is guaranteed by the sacrifice of His only Son.

With Christ's once-and-for-all sacrifice, the hand-cuffs on our wrists spring open. We are set free. Free from scrambling to balance the scale, free from the chains of trying to look good, be good enough, and measure up. The prison doors fly off the hinges, and we emerge with a heart spilled over with the only remaining sacrifices: thanksgiving, praise, and obedience born from the life-changing love of Christ for us.

"Through Him then, let us continually offer up a sacrifice of praise to God, that is, the fruit of lips that give thanks to His name. And do not neglect doing good and sharing; for with such sacrifices God is pleased" (Heb. 13:15–16).

And finally we understand what it means to be clothed with Christ.

LISTEN

"I have been crucified with Christ; and it is no longer I who live, but Christ lives in me; and the life which I now live in the flesh I live by faith in the Son of God, who loved me and gave Himself up for me" (Gal. 2:20).

"For the love of Christ controls us, having concluded this, that one died for all, therefore all died; and He died for all, so that they who live might no longer live for themselves, but for Him who died and rose again on their behalf" (2 Cor. 5:14–15).

LEARN

My hope is built on nothing less
Than Jesus' blood and righteousness.
I dare not trust the sweetest frame,
But wholly trust in Jesus' name.

His oath, His covenant, His blood
Support me in the whelming flood.
When all around my soul gives way,
He then is all my Hope and Stay.

When He shall come with trumpet sound,
O may I then in Him be found.
Dressed in His righteousness alone,
Faultless to stand before the throne.
On Christ the solid Rock I stand,
All other ground is sinking sand;
All other ground is sinking sand.

—Edward Mote

LIVE

What are some relinquishment moments for you when you gave what you couldn't afford out of love?

Which sacrifices come naturally to you? In which areas do you desire to grow?

When have you offered, out of obedience, a sacrifice of praise and then found your heart changed?

PART 6

THORNS IN THE GARDEN

In one section of our yard is this great stone pond. Several trees shelter it and provide shade, berries for birds, and cedar for scent. A pipe runs underground into the basin to allow for fish. Contour, texture, and height offer the possibility of creating a gorgeous setting, with rock-sprawling flowers like creeping phlox and shade-loving varieties of other plants.

Note the phrase, "offer the possibility of creating a gorgeous setting." This is in a perfect world. A world where someone tends the overgrowth more than once a year. One summer I picked one of the hottest, most humid days in Chicagoland's schizophrenic weather calendar to approach the pond. I'd have avoided it entirely, except that the hedges nearby along the fence line scratched the side of our car every time we exited the driveway.

Thistles with trunks like cornstalks encroached on the grass, vying for my unprotected skin, embedding themselves in my bare feet. Mosquitoes swarmed and attacked. Choking vines hung off the tops of the trees, taunting me from their high perches. New weed-trees had sprouted and grown several feet. Horrified, I rushed inside for long sleeves, jeans, shoes, thistle-proof gloves (which don't exist, I learned), and enough repellent to repulse a battalion of bugs. By the time I quit for the night—forced inside because of pitch darkness—sweat drenched every inch of cloth. I've disliked heat and its companion, sweat, since infancy and heat rash and high fevers that spiraled in seconds. I find no real virtue in sweat and easily regard it an offspring of the earliest garden problems.

Wagonloads of weeds later, I had scarcely made a dent in the thriving jungle. Here and there, ground appeared, freed of weeds so that the trees could breathe and receive rain. But the runners from the thistles also shot around underground, popping up and multiplying exponentially. Scratches lined my wrists and forearms and itching bumps where the poison from the thistles invaded my skin all reminding me of the original curse. This land so easily produces thorns and thistles, but the designer would have been appalled at its current state. This was not the blueprint the former owners drew up.

It is, however, a picture of my life, but not the life my original Designer intended. The soil of my soul becomes fertile land for every seed possible, and without tending, bears thorns and thistles. The jungle state of my spirit is a far fall from God's initial desire.

The curse came in after Adam and Eve ripped the fruit from the tree and tore their hearts away from dependence on God. God said to Adam, as a consequence of their disobedience, in Genesis 3:17–19, "Cursed is the ground because of you; in toil you will eat of it all the days of your life. Both thorns and thistles it shall grow for you; and you will eat the plants of the field; by the sweat of your face you will eat bread, till you return to the ground."

Sweat, bread, thorns—we will examine this trilogy as we move between the gardens.

22

SWEAT IN THE GARDEN

Although teenagers might disagree, with their huge sleep needs and a metabolism that lags behind growth spurts, work is not a curse. Work existed in Eden before Adam and Eve reached for that forbidden fruit. Adam's job description was clear: "Then the LORD God took the man and put him into the garden of Eden to cultivate it and keep it" (Gen. 2:15). While we may dislike our particular job, work has been part of the picture since creation.

The Scriptures read, "Cursed is the ground because of you; in toil you will eat of it all the days of your life" (Gen. 3:17). Embedded in the Hebrew word for *toil* are the adjectives *worrisome*, *grievous*, and *painful*, whereas the word in Genesis 2:15 for *cultivate* generally means "to work or till." "By the sweat of your brow" describes the process of wresting a living from the land, the difficulty—sweat—involved in moving from grain in the field to enjoying food on the table. Sweat and toil, a picture of the strain of tending the land, is the curse, not the tending itself. We will fight the soil and the condition of work for all our earthly lives.

God had already planted the garden; fruit swung ripe and heavy from the trees. Food in abundance surrounded them. But since Adam and Eve took matters into their own hands, *they* would be responsible for the labor and the now-backbreaking work of tending the land. In a paradise where there had been no sweat, Adam and Eve would scramble to keep up with the demands of a tedious and physically demanding job.

Even after Eden's gates closed and the angel stood guard, even after the curse went into effect, God directed the people into a land where all the work was already done for them. God, generous and forgiving, provided a land where the ground was tilled and planted, where vines groaned with grapes that grew large as grapefruits. "I gave you houses you didn't build and fields you didn't plant," God reminded the Israelites (see Deut. 6:10–12). But the people forgot God's good provision for them; they grew lax in their love of God and strayed; they were sent into captivity because they refused to follow God. They kept working the land despite the Lord's promise to provide for them if they offered a sacrifice with the first of the harvest, if they took one day off per week from their work to rest in God's presence and provision, if they took one year off out of every seven to let the land recuperate and to replenish their own trust levels. And so, because they kept working and quit trusting, the people were exiled from their land, and taken into captivity for seventy years. Decades later, with the land deeply rested, they would certainly tend and toil the neglected property, reliving the curse—they weren't hiking back into a cultivated and prepared land like the first time.

For us, work becomes a curse by feeding our addictive tendencies to put something else in the place of God, and work has just enough positive reinforcement to make us work hard. It also fits snugly into the slot designed for trust. Our inclination since the fall is to rely upon ourselves, and work is one more way we do this. The sweat of our brow— the difficulty and inherent benefits of hard work—constantly puts us in a quandary: In whom will we trust?

God reminded the Israelites, and now nudges us, "You must deny yourselves and do no work." To step back and away from work, to take a break and let God be in charge, handle the controls. We may find this more difficult than the work itself, because then we battle our compulsion to earn our way, to be independent and self-made.

Part of the work curse is that we're then tempted to focus on the wrong riches. We look at the paycheck, line it up against the bills, and then we clock in again because there's just not enough money. Yet in Ephesians 3:16–19, God urged us to get it straight; Paul prayed that God would grant us "according to the riches of His glory, to be strengthened with power through His Spirit in the inner man; so that Christ may dwell in your hearts through faith; and that you, being rooted and grounded in love, may be able to comprehend with all the saints what is the breadth and length and height and depth, and to know the love of Christ which surpasses knowledge, that you may be filled up to all the fullness of God."

If we move back to Genesis, the serpent tempts Adam and Eve with the promise of godlike knowledge. But here we find that *the love of Christ* surpasses real knowledge, and only then can we be full and complete. The curse of work finds its fulfillment not in riches or more work, but in the Christ, the one promised since Eden.

As a teenager, I worked in a bank, handing out little, cardboard, cat banks for dimes to eager children. I had saved dimes in the same way, until I realized I really was dealing with small change. Now, looking at Ephesians, we hone in even more. Focusing on the wrong riches, we live an impoverished spiritual life while working ourselves into a frenzy to make ends meet. God waits to pour riches—not dimes, not spare change—into my spiritual bank account, but I have zipped my heart tightly shut. I'm using a child's penny saver, and God has a vault full of treasures. I'm living the life of a spiritual miser, hoarding my pathetic grubby resources, and this shows up in my relationships with my husband, children, friends, and neighbors. And the Owner of the universe waits to *hand* me all the spiritual wealth possible.

Imagine the richest man in the world standing around with unlimited free cash for anyone who will hold out a hand. Would we wait in line with our wheelbarrows or semis, or be skeptical and stay home?

And our God, who owns the cattle on a thousand hills, all the resources in the entire world—the world itself—asks only for our trust, to focus on God, who promised to provide for us. Maybe it's one of the most important things we can learn from the law and its relationship to Eden's sweat-of-the-brow curse. And trust is a bridge between Eden and Gethsemane where we meet Christ. While we still sweat it out in between the two gardens, Jesus approached us from the other side, from the fulfillment.

Early in His ministry, Jesus drew fire from the religious ranks because He equated His work with the work of God. The listeners understood His meaning: He and the Father were one, equals. (They also wanted to kill Him for it.) But we find one of Jesus' most astounding assertions in John 17:4. He offered this prayer in the upper room, with His disciples present; Judas had just slipped away to rally the guards for the furtive arrest. Jesus said, "I glorified You on the earth, having accomplished the work which You have given Me to do."

He had finished the work? How had Jesus possibly accomplished the work already? He hadn't been arrested, tried, crucified, done battle with the Evil One, risen from the dead, appeared to the disciples or to the others, or ascended back to God. The world, in fact, was still a mess; the people were still under the rule of a foreign government; the disciples were mere hours away from abandoning all they'd been taught with such love and patience.

Jesus must have defined work differently than we do. To accomplish God's work doesn't mean we have finished everything on the world's to-do list. Jesus said, "This is the work of God, that you believe in Him whom He has sent" (John 6:29). This proves, indeed, to be work for us.

Though we still sweat and labor, Christ has labored for us. He accomplished the work God sent Him to do. Though painful and uncomfortable, we head to the garden, once again, to find the fulfillment of the work curse.

In the garden, in the thick darkness, Jesus agonized in private prayer, tormented over the coming sacrifice: "'Father, if You are willing, remove this cup from Me; yet not My will, but Yours be done.' Now an angel from heaven appeared to Him, strengthening Him. And being in agony He was praying very fervently; and His sweat became like drops of blood, falling down upon the ground" (Luke 22:42–44).

No more do we need to earn our place and find our meaning by the sweat of our brows. We are connected to God irrevocably through the work of Christ in the garden of Gethsemane, through the life of the risen Christ, who accomplished the work God gave Him. This same Christ, who sweated great drops of blood that we might know Him and the power of His resurrection, now intercedes between us and the Father, ever working for us, enabling us to transform every waking, working moment into a sacrament, an offering of praise, to the glory of God.

LISTEN

"The mystery . . . is now disclosed to the saints. To them God has chosen to make known . . . the glorious riches of this mystery, which is Christ in you, the hope of glory. We proclaim him, admonishing and teaching everyone with all wisdom, so that we may present everyone perfect in Christ. To this end I labor, struggling with all his energy, which so powerfully works in me. . . . And whatever you do, whether in word or deed, do it all in the name of the Lord Jesus, giving thanks to God the Father through him" (Col. 1:26–29; 3:17 NIV84).

LEARN

"It may be difficult for the average Christian to get hold of the idea that his daily labors can be performed as acts of worship acceptable to God by Jesus Christ. . . . We must offer all our acts to God and believe that He accepts them. Then hold firmly to that position and keep insisting that every act of every hour of the day and night be included in the transaction. . . . Let us practice the fine art of making every work a priestly ministration. Let us believe that God is in all our simple deeds and learn to find Him there. . . . Let every man abide in the calling wherein he is called and his work will be as sacred as the work of the ministry. It is not what a man does that determines whether his work is sacred or secular, it is why he does it. The motive is everything. Let a man sanctify the Lord God in his heart and he can thereafter do no common act" (Tozer, *Pursuit*).

LIVE

When do you find yourself resenting your work, working harder than should be necessary to make ends meet? How do you balance work and trust?

When have you experienced Christ coming alongside you, inviting you to put your neck into His yoke, that He might share your burdens? (See Matt. 11:28–30.)

When is your everyday work transformed into a lightness and joy, an offering to God? What happened to make that so?

23

BREAD IN THE GARDEN

God amply provided Adam and Eve with food in abundance; but as a result of their sin, they would eat bread "by the sweat of their face." Before their "independence day," God both planted and grew the food to sustain them. The curse meant that they would be responsible now for their own bread, their own rations.

Because Adam and Eve weren't content with the food God supplied, hunger began to grow in all of us for God. We would try, will try, to fill that hunger with many things, including food, but we would also mistake that hunger for a desire for power, possessions, and people. An insatiable craving for more would begin to characterize us, but the "more" can only be satisfied by God. Discontent would plague us, desires that could never be satisfied by material things. And our wandering eye would lust after all sorts of bread. We would find it nearly impossible to be satisfied by our work or the fruit of our labors. And because we were not content with the food God bestowed, we would be put in charge of the kitchen ourselves.

Between the gardens, the entire Jewish contingent packed their bags and girded up their loins for the great exodus out of Egypt. Before they fled, God stopped the people and set up a ritual: the staple of unleavened bread would quicken their memories of God passing over them to save them from the Egyptians. On the long march from slavery to the freedom of the Promised Land, God told the hungry and weary Israelites, "I will rain bread from heaven for you" (Ex. 16:4). And because God knew their tendency—and ours—to store up for tomorrow out of fear, to overwork so we don't have to trust, God said, "It's a daily deal. You'll gather only enough for the day. Not for two days, a week, or a year. Only on the day preceding the Sabbath will you gather enough for two days." And the people found out overnight that if they collected the cowards' rations, the leftovers grew moldy and writhed with maggots. Could this be a grim picture of the soul that doesn't trust the God who provides?

This miracle food could only come from Yahweh. And as a reminder, when laying out the design of the tabernacle and then the temple, God established the shewbread (or showbread) in the Holy Place. This "bread of the Presence" would always demonstrate God's gracious provision; in times of destitution and distress, it would jog the memories of the Israelites about God's bread in the wilderness. Deeper within the tabernacle, in the Most Holy Place or Holy of Holies, a pot of manna resided, a souvenir of God's dailyness (see Ex. 16:31–34; 25:16, 22, 30; Deut. 6:3). In spite of Adam and Eve's quest for independence and control, God's huge love for us leads us back; God never intended for us to hunger without finding sustenance and nurture in and through Him.

How amazing, the way God carries the people along— the bread in the wilderness, the offerings of bread, the pot of manna. Right out of the chute into ordained ministry, when Christ is whisked into the desert for tempting, He stands against Satan with the words, "Man shall not live on bread alone" (Matt. 4:4). Jesus lives it for us, showing us how to rely on Him and not on all the material things that woo us.

And is it any wonder that when the disciples said to Jesus, "Lord, teach us to pray," His words included, "Give us each day our daily bread" (Luke 11:1, 3)? Again Christ prompts us, like the Alcoholics Anonymous slogan, "One day at a time." He tells us, "Just trust me for this day; tomorrow has enough worries. Let's take today, friend" (see Matt. 6:34).

Jesus took five loaves of barley bread and multiplied them into food for thousands (John 6:9–13). Further on, Jesus urged His followers, "Do not work for the food which perishes, but for the food which endures to eternal life" (6:27). The disciples wanted to cling to Moses and the miracle manna-in-the-wilderness story, but Jesus corrected them: "It is not Moses who has given you the bread out of heaven, but it is My Father who gives you the true bread out of heaven. For the bread of God is that which comes down out of heaven, and gives life to the world" (6:32–33). And then, Jesus took it a step further, proclaiming, "I am the bread of life; he who comes to Me will not hunger" (6:35).

On the night before Christ's crucifixion, hours before His arrest in the garden of Gethsemane, the Lord Jesus gathered those who faithfully followed Him. They shared the Passover meal together in a small room, commemorating God's faithful deliverance from slavery in Egypt. "While they were eating, Jesus took some bread, and after a blessing, He broke it and gave it to the disciples, and said, 'Take, eat; this is My body'" (Matt. 26:26). He finished with, "Do this in remembrance of me" (Luke 22:19).

But the disciples didn't remember.

After the wretched events of the crucifixion, numbed by grief and dismayed by their broken dreams, two of Jesus' followers dragged down the road to Emmaus. A man appeared beside them, and they involved Him in their conversation as they rehashed the events of Golgotha and shook their heads in bewilderment. They walked together, two discouraged men and one whom they didn't recognize. The stranger started with Moses and then explained how it was necessary for the Christ to suffer these things. The day wore on. Nighttime crowded in and with it, surely, memories of darkness and horror. The two men said, "Stay with us. It's late." Luke 24:30 reads, "When He had reclined at the table with them, He took the bread and blessed it, and breaking it, He began giving it to them." When Jesus took the bread, blessed it, and offered the broken loaf to them, their eyes were opened. "He was recognized by them in the breaking of the bread" (Luke 24:35).

Even as baking bread creates a fragrance, luring us to the table, so the life of Christ and His words lure us to Him. His life becomes a fragrant aroma. Hunger for bread that endures, for eternal sustenance, growls within us until we acknowledge that only in Christ will we find our hunger satisfied. With the breaking of the Bread of Life, the curse of Eden is broken forever.

LISTEN

"I am the bread of life. Your fathers ate the manna in the wilderness, and they died. This is the bread which comes down out of heaven, so that one may eat of it and not die. I am the living bread that came down out of heaven; if any one eats of this bread, he will live forever; and the bread also which I will give for the life of the world is My flesh" (John 6:48–51).

LEARN

In Eden Adam and Eve learned, "Eat and die." In Gethsemane we learn, "Eat and live."

LIVE

What memories does the scent of baking bread bring to your mind?

What's your go-to food when you think you're hungry, but instead are tired, lonely, or frightened? What does discontent or anger do to your food or faith patterns?

When, in brokenness, have you found Christ to be your sustenance? How have you experienced the curse "by the sweat of your brow you will eat bread" being broken?

24

THE THORNS OF EDEN

For the gardener, for the human being, thorns and thistles are part of the package of tending the land. Adam and Eve's rebellion resulted in the curse of these hateful spined plants. After Eden, like dandelion fluff caught on the wind, thorns and thistles reproduced throughout the Old Testament, plaguing the Israelites in the form of enemies, scourging the land when the people left their plows and their God to follow the surrounding nations into captivity. But God promised the people deliverance from the thorns and thistles, and the New Testament reveals the fulfillment.

While Adam and Eve shivered in their garments of leaves, God said of the ground they would tend, "Cursed is the ground because of you. . . . Both thorns and thistles it shall grow for you" (Gen. 3:17–18). "Cursed" means the ground will no longer naturally offer up bounty, as God had originally promised. In their briarless world, Adam and Eve had no idea how wretched this curse would be, like moving from a putting green to a carpet of cactus skin. Shoes became mandatory apparel. They shed their barefoot innocence on exiting the first garden.

Ever since, we've reaped the consequences of seeds sown in Eden, and we still tread gingerly to avoid puncture wounds. Thorns and thistles pop up in the Old Testament between the two gardens in the forms of various enemies. Joshua warned the Israelites, as he prepared to die, that any unfaithfulness would result in the surrounding nations becoming "a whip on your sides and thorns in your eyes" (Josh. 23:13).

Then, when hauled off into captivity for their unfaithfulness by those surrounding nations, the Israelites returned to a land thick with thorns and thistles. They had to hack their way through the prickly, painful growth to once again plant and cultivate fruit. Though God promised in Ezekiel 28:24 that one day "there will be no more for the house of Israel a prickling brier or a painful thorn from any round about them who scorned them; then they will know that I am the Lord GOD," the Israelites would wait, and we would wait, for a long time for its fulfillment.

The curse presents such a picture of the neglected, sin-and-thistle-ridden heart. Hebrews 6:7–8 contrasts the porous soul that absorbs the rain and grows good fruit with the hard-souled person: "For ground that drinks the rain which often falls on it and brings forth vegetation useful to those for whose sake it is also tilled, receives a blessing from God; but if it yields thorns and thistles, it is worthless and close to being cursed."

What an act. We pretend to be fine and super-spiritual, to have control of our lives, even as we fondle the thorny branches and plait them into a garland to wear around our hearts. Our gardens burst, but not with fruit. Rather, thorns and thistles choke the ground.

The Scriptures tell us that the entire Roman cohort made a mockery of the assertion that Jesus was a king. They dressed Him up in a purple robe, wove a crown of thorns, and crushed it on His head, shouting "Hail, King of the Jews!" (Matt. 27:29; Mark 15:18; John 19:3), they spit at him and alternately knelt and bowed before Him and beat Jesus' thorn-circled head with a reed.

But Christ ended this part of the curse when those who mocked and betrayed Him rammed a crown of thorns onto His brow. In one more instance of turning cursing into blessing, those thorns of mockery from the enemies actually signaled the end of an era.

Isaiah prophesied of a time when "instead of the thorn bush the cypress will come up, and instead of the nettle the myrtle will come up, and it will be a memorial to the LORD, for an everlasting sign which will not be cut off" (Isa. 55:13). Eden's curse of thorns and thistles would be no more, their absence an eternal sign of the presence and power of God. By accepting that crown of thorns, and with His subsequent victory over sin and death, Christ had "put all His enemies under His feet" (1 Cor. 15:25) and crushed the head of the serpent. Christ died with the thorns of our sin piercing His brow, blood from those thorns staining His face, running into His eyes.

This is hard to hear. Especially in light of the thorns and thistles I allowed to grow in my home, in my garden-heart, this week. Thorns of anger, self-pity, and self-absorption. Thistles that barricaded me from loved ones, God, and friends. I cordoned off my soul and my joy by allowing those cursed weeds to live here, take root, and poison me. Amazingly, my thorns-and-thistles self does not alter Christ's work and provision for the end of the curse.

In every curse, God moves between us and total realization of the effects of the curse, providing and becoming bread, working by the sweat of our brows, fulfilling the work for us, cursing the land with thorns, wearing a mocking crown of thorns to signal their riddance. Never have we had to live totally without provision in the place of between; never have we fully been left to feel the entire ramifications of the curses. This is grace. This is Christ. This is Gethsemane and Golgotha and a crown of thorns.

LISTEN

"They dressed Him up in purple, and after twisting a crown of thorns, they put it on Him; and they began to acclaim Him, "Hail, King of the Jews!" They kept beating His head with a reed, and spitting at Him, and kneeling and bowing before Him. After they had mocked Him, they took the purple robe off Him and put His own garments on Him. And they led Him out to crucify Him" (Mark 15:17–20).

LEARN

No more let sins and sorrows grow,
Nor thorns infest the ground;
He comes to make His blessings flow
Far as the curse is found,
Far as the curse is found,
Far as, far as the curse is found.

—Isaac Watts

LIVE

Living with thorns and thistles becomes a choice. What hinders you in pulling out the barbs and prickly spines?

With which sins are you most comfortable? How have you learned to work around them, catering to them, allowing them to infest the ground of your heart?

What does the fulfillment of the curse of thorns and thistles mean for you?

PART 7

FAILURE IN THE GARDEN

Hollowness filled me. I left my friend's driveway and began the long trip home. I had failed in a relationship very important to me, and during the drive back, other failures crowded into the car, leering and ugly, reminding me of my global ineptitude. I translated a failed friendship into a lifetime of failure.

For all of us, failure in some way is guaranteed. The absence of failure suggests perfection, a condition that ceased to exist after that fateful day in Eden.

Even our definition of failure fails, for failure in the world's eyes means failing to acquire the success, power, wealth, or status deemed appropriate and even necessary, the amount of which is usually determined by others, not ourselves. Thus every shortcoming represents not our humanity, but our failure: a bounced check, a forgotten appointment, a messy house, a wayward child, a missed promotion, a demotion, a reprimand, a job loss, a broken marriage. All these tempt us to classify ourselves as failures.

Perhaps, instead, they are marks of our inheritance, of our descent from Adam and Eve. They are signs, indeed, of our insufficiency and our imperfection.

Failure fills the Scriptures: failed faith, morals, military campaigns, marriages, courage, societies, systems, and political reigns. Failure was rampant then as it is now. Anything less than perfection qualifies, and we consistently score well below that mark. The learning curve is steep and slippery, and on it we are all novice skiers on Dead Man's Ridge.

Part of the stigma of failure is that we see it from the world's eyes. From the vantage point of eternity, failure is necessary for redemption. Our failure puts us in the right place for God to triumph, for the saving life of Christ. Into the dark, dull void created by failure come the perfect life, faith, death, and resurrection of Jesus Christ.

25

FAILURE IN EDEN

In the infancy of creation, failure interrupted the rhythm of a perfectly synchronized world. It began with a story less familiar to us: the story of an angel, fallen from heaven, taking the form of a serpent (see Isa. 14:12–20). The failure quickly contaminated God's most precious creations: Adam and Eve.

Adam and Eve's failure, perhaps above all else, was a failure to trust God: His goodness, promises, and provisions. When they averted their gaze from God and toward themselves, when they ceased to listen to God's words and began to weigh truth on a different scale, they focused on what they didn't have rather than on what they did.

Anytime we turn our focus away from God and toward ourselves and the outspoken tauntings and temptings of another—in this case, Satan dressed in snakeskin—we're in danger. Whether we compare tangible goods or intangibles, comparison seldom leads to contentment, is rarely a positive tool, and sets us up for failure.

Adam and Eve failed when they began to trust their own abilities, to trust a wisdom and a measuring scale other than God's. We imitate our predecessors with nearly every breath.

Though businesses tell us, "Failure is part of the plan," failure is no badge of honor, just as the failure of Adam and Eve in the garden elicited no merits, no commendations, and no award for trying. Is this failure-babble rationalization, or might failure be a critical stepping-stone in the pathway to faith? How, exactly, is failure part of the plan, and is it truly helpful in today's society?

Avoiding failure seems about as easy as avoiding stepping on cracks on a mosaic-tiled floor. Plus, it's not all that consoling to remember that failure means we are alive. If failure is part of living in this world, regardless of whether we compare ourselves to others or simply go about our lives from day-to-day, how we deal with failure becomes crucial.

Our friends in Eden hid in the bushes and dressed in leaves to cover their failure. Their next reaction was blame. In failure, they cast blame, each laying downfall's cause at another's feet. This technique carries many people through their entire lives, as they justify their own shortcomings and failures by pointing to poor or inadequate treatment from others. By casting blame, however, we defer not only responsibility, but also growth. Father John Powell said, "Growth begins where blaming ends."

Like driving a stake into mud or hammering a nail into foam batting, failure too easily allows us to pound ourselves down, endlessly rehashing details, spiraling, infecting mood and thought, working our failure like worry beads. Every additional failure or mistake, however tiny, feeds into the pond of despair, confirming, like an endless echo in a canyon, our worthlessness.

Did an inability to let go of their failure haunt Adam and Eve for the rest of their lives? Did they replay the scene to one another in the dark of night, saying, "If only . . ."? When did they cease to blame each other for their own failure and come fully into God's presence, owning their past and turning it over to their Creator and Redeemer? I'm learning that the shorter the time between failure, blame, ownership, and relinquishment, the quicker I enter a place of grace, where God can bring fruit from my failures.

Interpreting others' failure toward us is different, however. How do we understand the failure of others? Do they, for instance, fail us because *we* are somehow worthy of better treatment? Do we translate their failure as rejection, indicative of our state or status or lack thereof? Do we feel shock, anger, surprise, or disappointment? Perhaps. And these feelings vary wildly; the more we are separated from our own fallenness and failings and the more we are disconnected from the truth about ourselves, the more we react to others' failures toward us.

But perhaps we swing toward denial. We need the illusion of another's perfection and refuse to believe a report of a loved one's infidelity or another's dishonesty or harmful behavior. We refuse the truth that we are all broken, incomplete, and prone to falls, stumbling, and flat-out failures.

When a loved one fails, it's easy to translate that failure as a reflection on our own image and worth. A child's trouble at school creates unease and feelings of failure in us as parents. A spouse's failure makes us look bad. When we cannot separate our feelings about ourselves from another's behavior, a sense of failure looms. Internalizing another's failure as our own becomes a dangerous pastime, because failure is global. No one is exempt. But it isn't our job to tell others how far they fall from the perfect ten, tempting as that might be. Because isn't that what we want to be certain of, in light of our failures—that others know for certain that they aren't perfect either?

So what is our ideal reaction to failure? Feeding on failure—our own or another's failure, or corporate or societal failure—is equivalent to drinking weed killer. Failure has a purpose just as weed killer does, but if misused it can be deadly.

LISTEN

"Though the fig tree should not blossom and there be no fruit on the vines, though the yield of the olive should fail and the fields produce no food, though the flock should be cut off from the fold and there be no cattle in the stalls, yet I will exult in the LORD, I will rejoice in the God of my salvation. The Lord GOD is my strength, and He has made my feet like hinds' feet, and makes me walk on my high places" (Hab. 3:17–19).

LEARN

"The mark of a broken leader is that he or she has a much deeper gratitude for the mercy and grace of our Lord. Unless we have wrestled with God in our own disappointment and come out limping, we are not broken. And it is only through authentic brokenness that we will be able to channel God's mercy and grace to our colleagues, coworkers, and congregations when they disappoint us or let us down. In our own unbroken strength, we are more apt to 'wash our hands' of people we deem unfit or who don't measure up to their calling. This hardness of heart leads to disaster in the ministry. We must unmask our own stubborn self-will and deal with it. Genuine brokenness is the only posture that prepares us adequately for the spiritual battles we face" (Umidi).

LIVE

When have you internalized another's failure as your own? When and with whom are you most vulnerable to this transference?

What is your typical reaction to failure? How do you give it over to God?

How and when has God brought fruit from your failures?

26

FAILURE BETWEEN TWO GARDENS

Don't we cut our teeth on competition? First steps, first grades, first team, first boyfriend or girlfriend, first job. The list continues. We want to be on the first-place team and take first place in any ranking, and we pass that gift on to our children. Here, no one sews badges on their vest for failure. The red ribbon always means almost, and bronze is never gold. Failure is comparison- and performance-based and disqualifies us instantly from first place. In America, as I once saw on a T-shirt, "Second place is first loser."

Pictures line shelves in one family's den. Six boys of varying ages peer out from the frames. Their father held strong ideas about competition, teamwork, and their tie-in with worth. The boys in front, dressed in their baseball uniforms, hold championship trophies. The boys in back, also in uniform, each hold up a sign that reads, "Loser." Does anyone really believe "it's how you play the game that matters"?

Failure trails Adam and Eve out of Eden, pockmarking the Scriptures. In a heavenly twist, though, failure instituted a change for many in the Old Testament. Abram got a new name after failure, becoming Abraham (Gen. 17:5). Liar and cheater Jacob used God's new name for him, Israel (meaning "he fights or persists with God"), after his beloved wife Rachel died (Gen. 35:16–20). David's moral failure with Bathsheba and his faithful processing of that failure ultimately led to a son who would lead Israel and from whom would come the Messiah. Moses never entered the Promised Land; Sarah laughed in the face of God's promise to have a child; Elijah sunk so low he could not get up from his despondency. In the New Testament, most of the disciples were dropouts, rejects from theological school. Thankfully, performance has nothing to do with God's love for people. These "failures" were the people with whom Jesus would entrust the most vital message of all time.

The failures of the people indeed riddle the Scriptures. Three truths, however, stand out, in contrast to our failure-prone existence.

God does not fail. Zephaniah 3:5 reads, "The LORD is righteous. . . . He will do no injustice. Every morning He brings His justice to light; He does not fail."

God's Word has not failed. In Joshua 23:14, Joshua reminded the Israelites (and us), "You know in all your hearts and in all your souls that not one word of all the good words which the LORD your God spoke concerning you has failed; all have been fulfilled for you, not one of them has failed."

Love never fails. The "love chapter," 1 Corinthians 13, lauds the attributes of love, not the least of which is found in verse 8: "Love never fails."

If one of God's characteristics is unfailing love and we are reminded continuously of God's faithfulness, then failure this side of heaven must bring about some redemption. Failure as a tool somehow brings us to a place of wholehearted (or wholer-hearted) trust. It then becomes part of the plan.

However, though we live in the age of "instant," instantly moving from failure's darkness into the brilliant daylight of lessons learned does not give us bouquets of praise. I've tried this with plants sheltered in a house all winter long. I move them into full sunlight unfiltered by glass, walls, and roof. First they sunburn, then they burn to ashes. I destroy a winter's worth of careful tending in one day.

One problem in our churches is that we leap too quickly from tragedy or trial to "Hallelujah! All is a blessing." If we process the pain of failure and our own human nature, somewhere in between, like the darkness between stark Friday and Easter Sunday, is this place of absolute loss, a place where we can say, with Job, "I brought nothing into the world and will take nothing out." This middle ground, cratered with doubt and shrouded with the clouds of reckoning, brings us, finally, to the end of ourselves. A place of utter reliance on and gratitude toward the God who never fails. Only then can we honestly finish Job's statement, "Blessed be the name of the LORD" (Job 1:21).

Failure is only successful (if we must use that term) if it brings us closer to the sufficiency of God. In failure we learn to rely not on our own abilities, but on the ability of God to bring about redemption of even the worst failure.

LISTEN

"Something crazy has happened, for it's obvious that you no longer have the crucified Jesus in clear focus in your lives. His sacrifice on the cross was certainly set before you clearly enough. Let me put this question to you: How did your new life begin? Was it by working your heads off to please God? Or was it by responding to God's Message to you? Are you going to continue this craziness? For only crazy people would think they could complete by their own efforts what was begun by God. If you weren't smart enough or strong enough to begin it, how do you suppose you could perfect it? Did you go through this whole painful learning process for nothing? It is not yet a total loss, but it certainly will be if you keep this up! Answer this question: Does the God who lavishly provides you with his own presence, his Holy Spirit, working things in your lives you could never do for yourselves, does he do these things because of your strenuous moral striving or because you trust him to do them in you? Don't these things happen among you just as they happened with Abraham? He believed God, and that act of belief was turned into a life that was right with God. Is it not obvious to you that persons who put their trust in Christ (not persons who put their trust in the law!) are like Abraham: children of faith? It was all laid out beforehand in Scripture that God would set things right with non-Jews by faith. Scripture anticipated this in the promise to Abraham: 'All nations will be blessed in you.' So those now who live by faith are blessed along with Abraham, who lived by faith—this is no new doctrine! And that means that anyone who tries to live by his own effort, independent of God, is doomed to failure. Scripture backs this up: 'Utterly cursed is every person who fails to carry out every detail written in the Book of the law'" (Gal. 3:1–10 MSG).

LEARN

"God, of your goodness give me yourself; you are enough for me, and anything less that I could ask for would not do you full honor. And if I ask anything that is less, I shall always lack something, but in you alone I have everything" (Julian of Norwich, *Revelations*).

"So, what do we do with sin? What is the humble response to our inevitable failure? Sin surely offends the heart of a holy God, so we never want to take it lightly.

How are we to ensure that it is dealt with, yet not give in to an unhealthy obsession with our own shortcomings? We must remember that we are spiritual beings who, for now, battle this body of flesh. We will sin. If we deny it, we are deceived; if we ignore it, we risk grieving the Holy Spirit (1 John 1:8; Eph. 4:22). Instead of trying to stir up a sense of sinfulness, we call upon God's Spirit to do His work. While we invite conviction on the basis of His righteousness, we cry out at the same time for restoration on the basis of His mercy. If we don't do this, we will end up being endlessly self-absorbed, counteracting the very work God seeks to do in our hearts. All sin, though grievous to our souls, should only serve to catapult us to His side, ravenous for a touch of grace" (Rhodes, *Taking*).

LIVE

What is your most humbling "failure"? How do you separate your sense of self from events of failure?

What have you learned about yourself in times of failure? About others? About your faith?

Where have you experienced God in the midst of failure?

27

FAILURE IN GETHSEMANE

How can our very faith hinge on the life, death, and accomplishments of One who the world determined a failure? Jesus, it seems, was a total failure: He failed in the eyes of everyone who knew Him. Socially, politically, culturally, and religiously, Jesus failed. He didn't marry, didn't have a home or a decent-paying job (all symbols of success), and wandered around like a transient. Christ lived a countercultural life, inverting all the norms of popular living, calling the meek blessed and the poor rich and the persecuted fortunate. Jesus failed to deliver Israel from political occupation, failed to convince even His disciples—His closest friends—of His plan and purpose. He didn't ride into the city on a white horse; He perched on an unbroken donkey. His life was exchanged for the life and freedom of a known criminal, Barabbas, and He died the death of a lowlife, hanging naked on a cross in full view of a mocking, spitting, hate-filled crowd.

I don't think that the disciples shouted TGIF as the guards battered their Lord and shattered their dreams. I don't think even God would call that Friday "good." Not from the world's eyes, using the system's measure of success. Nor did the disillusioned disciples cry, "Thank God for failure" as they watched all their hopes and plans die on a cross, the ultimate symbol of failure.

But God has never measured success or failure using the world's superficial standards. First Corinthians 1:27–29 says, "But God chose the foolish things of the world to shame the wise; God chose the weak things of the world to shame the strong. God chose the lowly things of this world and the despised things—and the things that are not—to nullify the things that are, so that *no one may boast before him*" (NIV, emphasis added).

If we're going to rely on superficiality, then Christ is a stumbling block, a failure. But if we are going to rely on God, then the cross of Christ, the life and death and resurrection of the Lord Jesus, stand like a lighthouse in the dismal darkness of all our failure. Ironically, into the failure that is death, death that began in Eden and should never have happened, God brings about fulfillment. Christ revolutionizes our idea of failure and redefines our notions of success. And He reminds us, who constantly fall into the potholes of failure and wrench emotional, spiritual, and relational ankles, that our brokenness, our weakness, even our failures become opportunities to be shaped and molded into the likeness of Jesus. In our failures, God can be glorified, when we turn them into opportunities for trust, growth, and new life.

In the intimacy of the upper room, with a donkey tethered outside, Jesus demonstrated to His followers the life of a servant by washing their feet, and He instituted what we now call the Lord's Supper. In this place of closeness and teaching, Jesus turned to Peter and said, "Simon, Simon, behold, Satan has demanded permission to sift you like wheat; but I have prayed for you, that your faith may not fail; and you, when once you have turned again, strengthen your brothers" (Luke 22:31–32). Peter flashed back with denial: "Lord, with You I am ready to go both to prison and to death!" (22:33). But Jesus knew. He knew that before the rooster crowed three times, Peter would deny ever knowing Him. Jesus knew that Peter would embrace the bitterest of failure and disillusionment, and Jesus knew that failure would not be fatal, but would rather become a tool to strengthen others. And the underscoring truth: Jesus didn't pray that Peter wouldn't fail, but rather, that his faith wouldn't fail.

Bold and brash, we, too, assert our faithfulness, only to hear the mocking call of the rooster, ridiculing our best efforts and reminding us not of our faith, but of our failure. And we, too, have the same choice that was available to Peter—once we have turned, we strengthen others.

Every time Elizabeth looked at her wedding ring, she heard that rooster. She remembered her vow to love, cherish, and remain faithful to her husband; she remembered the horrid stumbling, the affair she'd never intended to have, the relationship that promised heaven and delivered hell, and the bitter agony of moral failure. She remembered, too, her husband's love for her and his choosing her, again, and their choice to rebuild their marriage together in spite of her failure. And she remembered her choice to guide others on those dangerous coastlines away from the treacherous rocks of adultery by helping them understand the signs leading toward unfaithfulness and helping to build, rather than to destroy, their marriages. Like Peter, Elizabeth had a choice: to lose herself in her failure, to destroy her family, marriage, and faith, or to turn back toward God, honesty, and healing, and having turned, help others.

A pivotal moment follows Peter's failure, a life-changing, world-changing interaction. After the third person said, "Certainly this man also was with Him, for he is a Galilean too," Peter answered, his voice scraping over the rocks of denial, "Man, I do not know what you are talking about." The rooster crowed the third time before the last word had even died on Peter's tongue (Luke 22:59–60). The very next verse says, "The Lord turned and looked at Peter" (22:61).

Imagine the place of your greatest failure. Freeze the frame; feel the blackness, the hollow ugliness, the crushing disappointment, the self-hatred. Stay there. And then, in the courtyard of your failure, watch Jesus. Watch the One you love, the One you vowed to follow until death itself. Even as He heads into a place of torture and cru- cifixion, He turns. And meets your eyes. And offers you love. And you turn and remember His prophecy and strengthen others.

This, friend, is redemption. This is failure turned to glory for the sake of Jesus.

LISTEN

"And [the Lord] has said to me, 'My grace is sufficient for you, for power is perfected in weakness.' Most gladly, therefore, I will rather boast about my weaknesses, so that the power of Christ may dwell in me. Therefore I am well content with weaknesses, with insults, with distresses, with persecutions, with difficulties, for Christ's sake; for when I am weak, then I am strong" (2 Cor. 12:9–10).

LEARN

"It is God's choosing of us as His children that counts, not our betrayal of that choice. Hidden deeply in our actions of betrayal and faithlessness is the heart of a child, where a calling to be a child of God can still be heard. This capacity cannot be destroyed, either through failure or through self- inflicted death. For death does not have that power; it cannot kill what God has made alive. And what we have killed within ourselves, God can and will make alive through the life of His Son, Jesus Christ" (Anderson).

LIVE

When have you stood in the courtyard of failure? Describe your feelings.

Can you imagine yourself in Peter's place, meeting the Lord's eyes? What do you read in His gaze?

When has your faith failed because of your failure, and what can you do about that? Write a letter to God, describing your feelings of failure; wait with that, until you experience God's presence.

PART 8

EXILE FROM THE GARDEN

Burton Nelson writes about the great theologian Dietrich Bonhoeffer: "For the final two years of his life Bonhoeffer was a prisoner of the Third Reich, confined for the first eighteen months to . . . a cell room, six by nine feet, characterized by the simplest and humblest accommodation—a hard, narrow bed, a shelf, a stool, a bucket and a skylight window. This scarcely promised to be a setting in which some of the most creative theological thinking of the twentieth century could be born. It did, however, become precisely that as the months of confinement passed."

Exile reminds us of prisoners, people suffering unjustly because of "crimes against the government," but who are in actuality, or ultimately, imprisoned for their faith. Transferred from prison to prison, Dietrich Bonhoeffer bore witness to the joy of knowing and following Christ. He penned numerous letters as he lived out his faith within those walls, letters smuggled out by a sympathetic guard and eventually published as *Letters and Papers from*

Prison. Nelson reports that in one letter, Bonhoeffer wrote, "I am so sure of God's guiding hand that I hope I shall always be kept in that certainty. You must never doubt that I'm traveling with gratitude and cheerfulness along the road where I'm being led. My past life is brim-full of God's goodness, and my sins are covered by the forgiving love of Christ crucified."

Without the aid of others' writings and films, most of us can't imagine the horror of exile, nor the challenge exile represents to the spirit. Exile, though, often casts another in the role of judge. But must exile be crippling to the soul? Might it, as history demonstrates, actually be a means of great grace? We begin in the first garden with Adam and Eve, then travel through the Old Testament and into our own lives. We will move with Christ, exiled outside the City of David, into the final garden that ultimately has power to transform our own exile, our own alienation and separation from God.

28

ADAM AND EVE AND THE GARDEN EXILE

No longer innocent, after not only reaching for and eating the ripe, luscious, forbidden fruit, but after covering up their sin and hiding from God, Adam and Eve were in danger of living in permanent separation from their Creator. When they exiled God from their hearts, God, as an act of great grace and mercy, drove them—the word means thrust, hurled, expelled—from the garden of Eden. Though God had not withheld the fruit of the Tree of Life, now (lest they eat from that tree and live forever in their state of death) God cast them out. It sounds rough, harsh, and judgmental, but this exile would mean Adam and Eve's salvation. Their physical exile became a tangible reminder of their spiritual self-exile—forever they would remember Eden. The smell of rich earth, a flash of a bird's wing, a glimpse of a certain color, would pull them back to that place of perfection, back to the cause of their exile.

Adam and Eve also saw in the very next act of creation—their physical union and the birth of their first two children—the outworking of their exile. The consequences for choosing to live in separation from God meant suffering for their own children. The first Adam would go down in history as the one who exiled an entire world from God and set in motion a life of seeking and wandering for the entire human race.

Maybe they heard nostalgic stories of the first garden, but Cain and Abel would never know paradise. They would, however, know jealousy, coveting, revenge, and the logical conclusion to these when unrestrained: murder. Not unlike his parents, longing for what seemed better, reaching for what did not belong to him, Cain envied Abel's offering. Perhaps, too, Cain coveted Abel's relationship with God, his heart that sought after God. In taking his brother's life, murdering him in the field, Cain, like his parents before him, sought to become like God.

And thus the exile continued. The ripples, the separation, the isolation, the wandering down through the ages.

LISTEN

"The LORD builds up Jerusalem; He gathers the outcasts of Israel. He heals the brokenhearted and binds up their wounds" (Ps. 147:2–3).

LEARN

We live in our world as people in exile, forever wandering, moving, and separating from family and friends. Is there, beneath this permanent nomadic lifestyle, a longing for home, for the original place of safety? And in our state of constant seeking, are we becoming like Cain, taking the power of life in our hands, coveting the next better job, home, car, or income? And if so, if we become like Cain, who is Abel?

LIVE

What are the ramifications of exile in your own life? From childhood through adult years, when have you felt outcast and expelled?

How does exile impact your relationships with loved ones? With your God? With yourself?

When have you sent someone else into exile? Why? How did the exile end?

29

IN EXILE BETWEEN THE GARDENS

Exile from Eden inked the blueprint for a life of wandering exile. God told Adam and Eve's firstborn son, Cain, "You will be a vagrant and a wanderer on the earth." Cain reacted immediately, whining and protesting, even though he'd murdered his only brother: "My punishment is too great to bear! Behold, You have driven me this day from the face of the ground; and from Your face I will be hidden, and I will be a vagrant and a wanderer on the earth, and whoever finds me will kill me" (Gen. 4:12–14).

Even as Adam and Eve hid from God, so Cain's words, "From Your face I will be hidden," echo the horrid consequence of separation from God. This tears at my parent-heart, a heart that desires the very best for my children, and must have broken God's heart. But God, full of mercy, did not leave Cain helpless or unprotected. God marked him, designating him untouchable by enemies and ever reminding Cain of his Creator's gracious love and protection.

God does the same for us today—marks us as heaven's property, sealing us with the Holy Spirit of promise for our protection. God has not given Satan power over our souls. Through Christ, God promises us, "No temptation has overtaken you but such as is common to man; and God is faithful, who will not allow you to be tempted beyond what you are able, but with the temptation will provide the way of escape also, so that you will be able to endure it" (1 Cor. 10:13). Temptation haunted the story of Cain, but Cain refused to listen to the truth, the possibility of mastering sin. Before Cain killed his brother, God said, "If you do well, will not your countenance be lifted up? And if you do not do well, sin is crouching at the door; and its desire is for you, but you must master it" (Gen. 4:7).

Cain, apparently true to his destiny, finally settled in the land called Nod, which—no surprise!—means wandering or exile (Gen. 4:16). Every day of his life, the very dust of the earth beneath his feet reminded him of his choice, marked by the decision to take life rather than to honor it.

The word for "driven" in Genesis 4:14 is used when God drove Cain's parents from Eden: Adam and Eve's son was also thrust out, expelled from the family farm. This word is again used to describe God's action in the lives of the Israelites: God promised to "drive out" the enemies before them, to expel the Hivites, Canaanites, and Amorites from the Promised Land. The Israelites, however, struck a bargain with some of those enemies and allowed the enemies to live among them.

God is quite willing to go before us, as with the Israelites, to drive out the enemies and to clear a path for us. Like Cain and the Israelites, we choose exile and alienation when we allow enemies to camp in our garden, to pitch their tents in our soul's soil. The stakes often are pounded deeply into our psyche, whether emotions gone awry like anger turned to rage, or coveting or fear, which leads us either to build up treasures on the earth or to hide.

We're comfortable with our enemies, fraternizing, making treaties. "I'll cover for you. Stay as long as you want, just don't show your face to anyone else." Or our enemies pretend a friendship, and bargain with us, "I'll let you keep living as long as you keep our relationship—this secret, this sin—between us." Like violence, pornography, a two-level lifestyle (pious at church and different at home), secret addictions like alcohol, painkillers, or food—these are covert relationships that we allow to live, like mold in a damp basement, in the hidden places of our hearts.

God would drive them out, exile them, but instead we choose to live in a personal exile, for the splintered life is a life of exile from God.

Hundreds of verses in the Old Testament warn about uncleanness, which separates us from God. The rigorous fastidiousness—eating the right food; not touching "unclean" people, animals, or substances; not engaging in unclean acts—was about relationship. God, who is holy, couldn't walk about their camp with its uncleanness. Uncleanness exiles us, and God wants to be part of our lives.

No uncleanness was allowed in the camp, Holy City, temple, or tabernacle. A dead body was considered unclean, so elaborate arrangements were made in case a priest died in the Most Holy Place. If the bells on the ends of the priest's garments stopped jingling, the priest outside the doorway tugged on the pull rope, dragging the dead body outside the Holy Place. Death was not to be part of the Holy City or the Holy of Holies, just as it wasn't intended for Eden.

The Israelites carried waste outside the camp, and later outside the city when Jerusalem was built, where they disposed of it. People with infectious diseases cried out, "Unclean! Unclean!" if someone passed by, signaling that no one could touch them. The Scriptures say, "As long as they have the disease they remain unclean. They must live alone; they must live outside the camp" (Lev. 13:46 NIV).

How often do we exile others after judging them unclean? We exile others emotionally, alienating them when they do something less-than-perfect or different than we expect or if they treat us as somehow less than we deserve. Perhaps they dress inappropriately or don't look good enough to be with us or their mannerisms embarrass us so we exclude them. We send them outside the camp, becoming like God to avenge our hurt.

Or we exile ourselves, pulling away in self-judgment, pushing others from us. Unclean! Stay away from me! We become emotional lepers, living in the outhouse instead of carrying our shame, anger, and hurt to Christ.

Maybe we exile our children when they don't measure up. Our neighbor, the pastor, a coworker, the cashier—no one is exempt from our perfection-seeking, judgment-rendering exile.

Exile can transform, however. When exiling the Israelites for their sinful ways, their idolatry, God intended that exile move them to repentance and change. Exile becomes a type of spiritual formation, a place where our losses and alienation wean us from dependency on all, save God.

Hezekiah's son, King Manasseh, was so evil that blood ran in the streets of Jerusalem (2 Kings 21:16), so evil that God removed him from the throne and exiled him to Assyria, a country renowned for torturous treatment of prisoners. Exile transformed him, breaking his idolatrous heart and leading him back to God. In her book *Among the Gods*, Lynn Austin describes Manasseh's anger and then desperation while in exile, a desperation descending into near madness. When God showed him the wickedness in his heart, Manasseh found relief only in the loving presence and undeserved forgiveness of God. We know this because of the changes he instituted after returning from exile. Second Chronicles 33:15–16 says, "[Manasseh] got rid of the foreign gods and removed the image from the temple of the LORD, as well as all the altars he had built on the temple hill and in Jerusalem; and he threw them out of the city. Then he restored the altar of the LORD and sacrificed fellowship offerings and thank offerings on it, and told Judah to serve the LORD, the God of Israel" (NIV).

While in exile, we have a choice. The best choice, of course, is to turn to God and allow grace to heal and transform our exile, helping us to bloom in the desert, making true the Scripture, "Their life will be like a watered garden" (Jer. 31:12). Exile transforms us, then transforms the world around us.

LISTEN

"When they are in the land of their enemies, I will not reject them, nor will I so abhor them as to destroy them, breaking My covenant with them; for I am the LORD their God. But I will remember for them the covenant with their ancestors, whom I brought out of the land of Egypt in the sight of the nations, that I might be their God. I am the LORD" (Lev. 26:44–45).

LEARN

"[Many] well-known dissidents from Russia and other repressive regimes . . . had a tremendous influence on the church and even society at large while they were in prison. But what happened to them once they were released? Aleksandr Solzhenitsyn moved to America, became a millionaire, made a couple of good speeches while the people were still listening, and then lost his influence. I'm glad that he has now returned to Russia, but I fear his opportunity to make a real difference there may have passed" (Brother Andrew).

LIVE

What enemies do you allow to live in your garden? How can you relinquish them, allowing God to drive them out and exile them?

What promises of God comfort and encourage you?

Might this be a time of exile, either self- or other-imposed? How might God desire to transform you during this season?

THE FINAL EXILE

Why do so many paintings portray Jesus as weak and emaciated? After reading and rereading the Gospels, I see only the steel-like strength of His faith, character, and endless love. Never in history has a man of such determination lived. And Jesus was no foreigner to exile. An angel warned Joseph in a dream that Herod sought their newborn Son, and said, "Get up! Take the Child and His mother and flee to Egypt" (Matt. 2:13). This family escaped by night to Egypt, where they stayed until Herod's death.

In another dream, an angel appeared to Joseph and instructed him to take his family back to Israel. But in Israel, Joseph learned that Herod's son reigned over Jerusalem and was afraid to go there. Again, God warned him in a dream to flee, this time to Galilee.

Then, after years of apprenticeship with His father, exile inaugurated Jesus' ministry. A similar Greek word for "drove out" in the Old Testament is used for Jesus being driven out, thrust out, hurled into the wilderness (Mark 1:12).

Jesus knew life on the run; exile was woven into the fabric of His experience. Echoing the strains of Eden's departure, we hear His words to a scribe, "The foxes have holes and the birds of the air have nests, but the Son of Man has nowhere to lay His head" (Matt. 8:20).

An outcast himself, Jesus feared no reprisal from touching a fellow outcast. When a leper came to Him, bowed down to Him, and said, "Lord, if You are willing, You can make me clean," this Son of Man didn't scream, "Unclean! Unclean!" No. Christ stretched out His hand, touched him, and said, "I am willing; be cleansed" (Matt. 8:2–3).

Jesus also drove out, cast out, and ejected the vendors who wanted to pollute the temple, distract the worshipers, and pervert their relationship with God. "You cannot buy that restoration, that forgiveness, with God, nor the proper sacrifice," He seemed to say. Christ alone could purchase that relationship, securing it for all eternity.

But while Adam and Eve were exiled *from* the garden of Eden, Christ was ultimately exiled *to* the garden, to Gethsemane, where enemies arrested Him and led Him away to the "Place of a Skull"—Golgotha.

Christ was crucified "outside the camp," exiled from the Holy City, the City of David, the place where His followers hoped He would reign. Christ was cast out by friends, rulers, religious people, and ultimately God. Christ, the second Adam (1 Cor. 15:45) also had to be exiled, driven out of the camp, that He might conquer all the enemies. "For [Christ] must reign until He has put all His enemies under His feet" (1 Cor. 15:25).

Jesus *chose* exile, voluntarily going outside the camp. Who can understand that commitment, that love, that overwhelming . . . what? Integrity? Strength? And would we accompany Christ into exile, meeting Him outside the camp, sharing His disgrace? Only if we are willing to be changed by that exile.

May God help us to be willing to change, to be transformed as a result of meeting Christ in exile. For Christ suffered, outside the city gate, bearing our reproach, our uncleanness, that we might never again know alienation and exile from God. Though the exile's mirror shows an emaciated, skeletal face—the face of the living dead— the mirror of the soul reflects a joy undaunted by starvation and deprivation, a heart fed and filled by the continual presence and comfort of God in Christ Jesus.

LISTEN

"The high priest carries the blood of animals into the Most Holy Place as a sin offering, but the bodies are burned outside the camp. And so Jesus also suffered outside the city gate to make the people holy through his own blood. Let us, then, go to him outside the camp, bearing the disgrace he bore. For here we do not have an enduring city, but we are looking for the city that is to come" (Heb. 13:11–14 NIV).

LEARN

"'The people who love . . . are the most revolutionary people on earth. They are the ones who upset all values; they are the explosives in human society.' But they are also those 'whom they want to get rid of, whom they declare an outlaw, whom they kill'" (Bonhoeffer, *Testament*).

LIVE

How are we called to bear Christ's disgrace outside the camp? When have you experienced the disgrace of exile?

What does it mean to you, to be transformed by meeting Christ in exile?

What does exile cost you? When have you paid the price, and what has been the fruit of exile?

PART 9

SUFFERING IN THE GARDEN

Rain slashed against the blank windowpanes like needles hitting metal. The darkness and gloom outside mimicked the darkness inside my soul. In the hospital waiting room, I wrestled with the intense physical and emotional pain loved ones were experiencing. I had to be careful not to close my eyes. Otherwise, in the dark, the tears rushed to the sealed shutters and pressed their way through, bullies with a shoulder push.

The next day, my young son and I walked to the playroom on the children's floor of the hospital. We both stopped to admire a toddler in a yellow T-shirt that reached nearly to the floor. She wore matching fuzzy, yellow footies that glowed against the floor's linoleum. Her beaming smile charmed and warmed our cold, tired, and frightened hearts. Only on the way back to the room did I see the five-inch scar wrapping over the child's head and down the side of her scalp.

So much pain. My own is only a microcosm; the pain I feel for others a drop in the huge ocean of suffering in this world. Since the seed of suffering was planted in Eden ("I will make your pains in childbearing very severe; with painful labor you will give birth to children. . . . Through painful toil . . ." [Gen. 3:16–17 NIV]), its roots have wrapped around the lives of individuals. In this world, pain isn't an elective course. Suffering seems to be a curriculum requirement to get our degree, and it's both a by-product of our faith and a by-product of garden choices.

31

ROOTED IN EDEN

As suffering works through the soil of our lives, it assumes different forms. The Voice of the Martyrs group (persecution.com) has workers in sixty-four nations, restricted and/or hostile to Christianity. Sixty-four nations where people are persecuted for their faith. But at this time in history, few of us in the Western world experience actual persecution for our beliefs, at least not the outright torture and oppression of many faraway relatives in the body of Christ.

In some countries, a convert to Christianity can expect estrangement, deportation, or even death at the hands of family members. In other nations, faith in Christ means slavery, mutilation, and genocide. Some experience less drastic but still real consequences when friends, family members, or associates at church see them take a stand for integrity or holiness and mock or ostracize them. For example, when Jeremy refused to gossip about the pastor with other church staff, they excluded him, undermining his ministry and reputation.

Perhaps we aren't persecuted outright for belief in Christ, but other types of suffering also sprout from the seeds sown in Eden. Physical pain and illness, emotional or psychological anguish, and spiritual crises also create genuine suffering in our lives and should not be minimized.

Liz, for example, endures debilitating migraines and blindness as a result of a pear-sized tumor that killed her optic nerves. Chronic fatigue syndrome leaves Michael constantly exhausted, battling depression, and shelving his dreams because of a flat-lined energy level. David's diagnosis of bipolar depression followed months of manic spending and several suicide attempts and wreaked havoc on his marriage and finances; ultimately, he changed jobs and moved his family across the country to start over.

Pain is real, and comparing pain is a dangerous and futile process. How tempting to look at another's suffering and say, "Yeah, I should have it so easy! You wouldn't believe what I'm going through." Or our pain doesn't measure up to another's, so we negate our own. Pain is pain, and it's interpreted by our spirit and body as pain regardless of the degree, severity, or type of suffering. To minimize the agony of a breaking marriage because the neighbor's battle with cancer seems more serious puts the heartbroken in danger of a downward spiral. The husband whose wife left him for another man has valid pain; another's real suffering shouldn't diminish his trauma or force him into denial or even shame.

To avoid that danger, we can recognize our bodies' attention-getting symptoms: taut nerves, tears, headaches, short tempers, out-of-proportion reactions, forgetfulness, fatigue, depression, binge eating, inability to sleep, or sleeping too much. Richard Swenson writes in *Margin*, "Our pain . . . is actually an ally of sorts. In the hurt is a help. Pain first gets our attention—as it does so well—and then moves us in the opposite direction of the danger."

LISTEN

"Therefore you too have grief now; but I will see you again, and your heart will rejoice, and no one will take your joy away from you. . . . These things I have spoken to you, so that in Me you may have peace. In the world you have tribulation, but take courage; I have overcome the world" (John 16:22, 33).

LEARN

"Man has to suffer. When he has no real afflictions, he invents them" (Martí).

LIVE

When and how has suffering demanded your attention?

What is your typical response to suffering or pain? To another's suffering or pain?

How do you compare your pain or suffering with another's? What would be a helpful response?

32

PITFALLS OF PAIN

When suffering gets our attention, what do we do with it? Numerous pitfalls exist when we try to face our pain.

We idolize our pain. Donna created an idol of her pain. She was terrified to come close to its fire, but the flames crept ever closer. She feared that it would destroy her life, burning her beyond recognition, so much that she couldn't live with the charred remains. If she faced it, she feared the suffering would consume her. If only she could dig trenches and saturate them with water and stand her ground, but pain so scarred her soul that she fabricated elaborate stories to push away reality. In this way, she circled her pain, bowing down to it, idolizing it.

We alienate others and isolate ourselves. Brendon's physical suffering was so intense that he alienated the very people he loved the most, the people who could actually help him work through his crippling illness. To isolate himself, he created conflict in his relationships and then nursed his hurt feelings, deflecting his attention from the real issue—his pain and decreasing mobility and independence.

We abandon progress. Too much rummaging around in the basement of our pain could lead us to abandon the building process. When Israel was in exile, held captive in Babylon, King Cyrus decreed that the Israelites could return to Jerusalem to rebuild the temple. Nearly fifty thousand people responded and set about the restoration. But the ruling government hired deconstruction specialists, who dug up the history of Israel and reported to the king, "If that city is rebuilt and the walls are finished, they will not pay tribute, custom or toll, and it will damage the revenue of the kings" (Ezra 4:13). So the king issued a decree to halt the building, and "the people of the land discouraged the people of Judah, and frightened them from building" (4:4). Progress was halted because the enemy excavated the past.

When we face our suffering and begin rebuilding our lives on this new foundation, it forces others to change how they relate to us. Their perception and treatment of us inevitably changes, and possibly not for the better. Their reaction may be a wrecking ball to our spirit. Hopefully, though, we encourage others to grow by our courageous response.

Plus, pain is messy. It is rarely a clean-cut event, with a beginning, middle, and end. Initially, it may even bring out the worst in us. Jan Dravecky, writing about her own struggle with depression during her husband's battle with cancer, says, "Suffering is not tidy, because suffering is a purifying process, a process of cleansing out impurities. When suffering causes impurities to rise to the surface, naturally we are going to see the worst of people. Their selfishness is going to come out, their wrong priorities are going to become apparent, and they are not going to be able to mask their sinfulness anymore."

Pain also leads us to feelings of worthlessness. Henri Nouwen reminds us that one of the blessings of pain is that in its midst we are wrapped in God's loving, affirming presence. We, unfortunately, are tempted to believe instead that brokenness points to our worthlessness: "Once we are in touch with the blessing, we can live with our brokenness in a very different way. The great question of ministry and the spiritual life is to learn to live our brokenness under the blessing and not the curse. . . . Many live their brokenness under the curse. They don't think they are loved, or held safe, and so when suffering comes they see it as an affirmation of their worthlessness."

Other pitfalls include the glacial slowness of the process of pain and the reality that suffering continues in one form or another. My friend says, "Our lives are like the Morton Salt commercial. When it rains, it pours." And finding the power of pain is largely a matter of perspective; it's called hindsight.

LISTEN

"But we have this treasure in earthen vessels, so that the surpassing greatness of the power will be of God and not from ourselves; we are afflicted in every way, but not crushed; perplexed, but not despairing; persecuted, but not forsaken; struck down, but not destroyed; always carrying about in the body the dying of Jesus, so that the life of Jesus also may be manifested in our body" (2 Cor. 4:7–10).

LEARN

"I wanted to have every kind of pain, bodily and spiritual, which I should have if I were dying, every fear and assault from devils . . . for I hoped that this would be profitable to me when I should die, because I desired soon to be with my God" (Julian of Norwich, *Showings*).

LIVE

Which pitfalls of pain have you encountered? How do you avoid the pitfalls?

How have you experienced God's presence in painful times and their pitfalls?

Talk about the "treasure in earthen vessels" from 2 Corinthians 4:7–10. How might this shape the way you handle pain?

POWER OF PAIN

A conversation with our then eight-year-old highlighted the truth in the overused axiom, "No pain, no gain." Many nights Zak awakened us, moaning from the pain in his legs and shins. One morning I glanced up when he thundered down the stairs for school. I hugged him good morning, and said, surprised, "You've grown a foot!"

"Must be those growing pains," he said, standing up soldier straight. I laughed. "Do you think they *were* growing pains, Mom?"

"Could be. I've heard they can be quite painful."

"I hope so," he said. "I don't want to go through all that pain for nothing. Might as well grow through it."

Whatever the type of pain, we can be bound by it, or we can harness its power, allowing it to lead us into places we would never otherwise enter. Pain has focusing value, but its value depends on our point of focus. To concentrate on the agony is like looking in a Magic Eye poster for the hidden picture to appear and seeing only the abstract, blurring particles. To see the hidden picture, we have to focus on a point somewhere beyond the collage-like pieces. Lamaze, one method of natural labor and delivery, uses the same principle. In Lamaze the woman in birthing pain trains to breathe evenly and focus not on the pain, but on a point beyond the pain, outside of herself, a place of beauty or interest.

Paul's words in 2 Corinthians 4:17–18 make sense: "For momentary, light affliction is producing for us an eternal weight of glory far beyond all comparison, while we look not at the things which are seen, but at the things which are not seen; for the things which are seen are temporal, but the things which are not seen are eternal."

Pain is a lesson in growth, grace, and trust, focusing on the unseen. In suffering we learn to focus on the *end* and not the means. Christ didn't allow anguish to separate Him from God or to deflect His focus. To benefit from pain, we must learn from it—about ourselves and about God. Adversity teaches us. A rabbi in Lynn Austin's book *Faith of My Fathers* responds to his anguished pupil's questions about suffering: "You may certainly question Yahweh, but ask the right questions. . . . Ask Him what He wants to teach you through this suffering. Ask which of your faults, like pride or self-sufficiency or self-righteousness, He's trying to purge from you. Ask which of His eternal qualities, like love and compassion and forgiveness, He wants to burn into your heart. Yes, go ahead, ask questions! Ask why He gave you the talents and gifts that He did—your excellent mind, your ability to lead others. Ask Him what He wants you to do with your life."

Perhaps we've been asking the wrong question. Rather than scrabbling around in the surface dirt and pebbles, demanding "Will I be healed?" we need to dig more deeply, asking, "Will I be whole? Will I be holy?"

In her book *In My Father's House*, Bodie Thoene tells of Ellis, an American soldier wounded in World War II, who said, "Life is hard." His companion, Theo Lindheim, a German fighter pilot, said, "Yes. And that is the truth of it. You have lost your leg [for a better world] and the world is still a toilet. Your loss changes nothing, means nothing, unless it makes you a better man. This is why we suffer. Like a fire, it burns the filth of our souls away."

We experience the power of pain when we learn to focus on God, grip tightly to God's hand, and walk through growth together.

LISTEN

"For He has not despised nor abhorred the affliction of the afflicted; nor has He hidden His face from him; but when he cried to Him for help, He heard" (Ps. 22:24).

"The Spirit of the Sovereign LORD is on me, because the LORD has anointed me to proclaim good news to the poor. He has sent me to bind up the brokenhearted, to proclaim freedom for the captives and release from darkness for the prisoners" (Isa. 61:1 NIV).

LEARN

"I do not like this bitter path before me. Compliance to my own suffering galls me, but I know it is important for me to bow my head before this pain. . . . There is a work of God going on in me, and I must not use up the energies I need to hold myself constant to an attitude of surrender. I must use this little season of pain to learn how to identify with Christ's suffering. Yet admittedly, I slouch toward Jerusalem, I sleep in Gethsemane, I stand silent at Golgotha" (Mains).

LIVE

What has your pain or suffering taught you about yourself? About God?

How have you chosen to focus?

Where have you seen the power hidden beyond the pain?

34

FRUIT FROM SUFFERING

Though suffering is rooted in a life far below the life God imagined and designed us for, when we choose to let suffering fertilize and enrich our lives—choosing to be holy, as God is holy—our Gardener brings forth fruit, not only in our lives, but also in the lives of others. Seeing suffering as discipline, we wait more patiently for the fruit of discipline, a harvest of righteousness and peace (Heb. 12:11).

Waiting forces us to rely on God. In Sunday school, Will said, "Desperation opens the door for faith in a way that nothing else does." Teresa nodded, adding, "My faith has been built by my suffering. We're more willing to hear what God has to say when we're in despair." This affirms Paul's words in 2 Corinthians 1:9: "But this happened that we might not rely on ourselves but on God, who raises the dead" (NIV).

Joseph said when he named his son Ephraim, after triumphing in spite of being sold into slavery, "God has made me fruitful in the land of my affliction" (Gen. 41:52). This fruitfulness in our own lives extends, then, into the lives of others. "You intended to harm me," Joseph told his brothers later, "but God intended it for good to accomplish what is now being done, the saving of many lives" (50:20 NIV).

Suffering becomes significant when it impacts others through us. A woman who was sexually abused as a teenager now helps others with similar backgrounds. She determined to share her secret shame, so others might heal.

"You have been damaged," writes Dan Allender. "But you have great hope. The mercy of God does not eradicate the damage, at least not in this life, but it soothes the soul and draws it forward to a hope that purifies and sets free. Allow the pain of the past and the travail of the change process to create fresh new life in you and to serve as a bridge over which another victim may walk from death to life."

Suffering, in between the two gardens, invites us to be changed, to love and live with the determination of Christ, to rely on God and share God's grace, and to intercede for others who are suffering or persecuted.

LISTEN

"'My son, do not make light of the Lord's discipline, and do not lose heart when he rebukes you, because the Lord disciplines the one he loves.' . . . Endure hardship as discipline; God is treating you as his children. . . . God disciplines us for our good, in order that we may share in his holiness. No discipline seems pleasant at the time, but painful. Later on, however, it produces a harvest of righteousness and peace for those who have been trained by it" (Heb. 12:5–7, 10–11 NIV).

LEARN

"In adversity our intellectual knowledge becomes actual knowledge. 'Even though I walk . . . through the valley of the shadow of death, I will fear no evil, for you are with me. . . .' And now that you and I are walking through that valley we will learn if it is true. Adversity is the testing ground of our faith. God has to risk losing you forever to your anger and bitterness in order to have you for His true son. Anyone can believe and sing praises on the temple mount when the sun is shining, but true praise is sung in the darkest valley when the Accuser tells you to curse God for making you suffer so much pain. If you can still praise your Father's goodness, even in the darkness, then you are His son indeed" (Austin, *Faith*).

LIVE

When have you experienced the significance of suffering?

How has it deepened you? What does it mean, to make you "more like Christ"?

In what ways can your travail become a means of extending the love and grace of God to others?

35

THE END OF SUFFERING

A lovely woman with huge waves of blond hair swept into the refreshment room at a retreat. She navigated over to the coffee cart, and we nodded, smiling at one another. Then her story spilled out. Her father died, she found her mother dead at the breakfast table three months later, and right after burying her mother, her husband had a heart attack. After being released to return to work, he had a second coronary and died. All within nine months. Issues with his children from a previous marriage compounded her grief and pain. All this left her alone. Very alone.

We moved into the room where our group worshiped. The only two chairs available were side by side. As we sang and prayed, I glanced at my neighbor. Her head was bowed, tears streamed down her face. Emphasizing her loneliness, her arms wrapped around herself, clutching her rib cage, maybe to hold herself together against the explosive grief.

So many unanswered questions about suffering. Looking back through journals, I find example after example, life after life, where suffering seems endless, brutal, and needless. And yet, through our questions, we must somehow content ourselves to live in the unease of mystery, to live without all the answers, to make our temporary home in the unknown.

Ultimately, we move closer to the garden of Gethsemane when we embrace the truth of Isaiah 53:5: "The punishment that brought us peace was on him, and by his wounds we are healed" (NIV). In some mysterious and inexplicable way, Christ's work on the cross completes our sufferings. First Peter 2:24 says, "He Himself bore our sins in His body on the cross, so that we might die to sin and live to righteousness; for by His wounds you were healed."

One fact is irrefutable: Suffering is finite. One glorious day, we'll live in a place of fulfillment, where Christ's struggle in Gethsemane, His suffering in Jerusalem and on Golgotha, and His subsequent victory over darkness and evil will catch up to our own lives. In heaven, God promises to "wipe away every tear from [our] eyes; and there will no longer be any death; there will no longer be any mourning, or crying, or pain; the first things have passed away" (Rev. 21:4).

LISTEN

"So the ransomed of the LORD will return and come with joyful shouting to Zion, and everlasting joy will be on their heads. They will obtain gladness and joy, and sorrow and sighing will flee away. I, even I, am He who comforts you" (Isa. 51:11–12).

LEARN

O Joy that seekest me through pain,
I cannot close my heart to thee;
I trace the rainbow through the rain,
And feel the promise is not vain,
That morn shall tearless be.

—George Matheson

"The disciple has no need to look for suffering; each disciple has a particular cross awaiting him. The sufferings of the Christian are defined by Christ—they involve, for example, bearing the sins of others in a ministry of forgiveness. It is not the suffering but the fellowship with Christ that is important; that is why the way of the disciples is seen as joyful and triumphant" (Willmer).

LIVE

What questions do you have about suffering? Your own? Another's? About Christ's fulfillment of suffering?

When do you most doubt? When do you most trust?

When have you experienced the truth of the hymn's words, "O joy that seekest me through pain"?

PART 10

LIFE IN THE GARDEN

The Gardener's plan for life from the seeds of death sown in Eden never ends. God brings life to the tired and withered, hope to those without hope, meaning and purpose to those floundering. God finds us in our lostness, and guides us into a new, fruitful place.

God's choices were always for life, forever; yet ours, because of those seeds, naturally lean toward death. Anytime we take life into our own hands, we choose death, exile, and separation from God. Look at Adam and Eve, snagging the fatal fruit, hoping for godlike powers. If only they'd understood that they were made in the image of God! They didn't need to grasp and grapple with death. The waves of their death-choices spread from Eden through history, spilling into the life of Christ in Gethsemane.

But God's plan always for life pounds triumphantly as we enter the garden, with the new tomb carved from the rock. In our own lives, we find the miracle of miracles. Into this body of death, Christ has seeded His very own life, breathing into us the air of salvation and newness of spirit.

EVE IN EDEN

The hush of a new day rests over creation. In the predawn silence, the first bird awakens, and a note, then two notes, break the stillness. A melody begins, a song of life and love to the Creator. The music crescendos. A man enters into the symphony, a being never before seen, envisioned only by the Trinity in heaven. He goes about his work, examining each living creature, but shakes his head at every one. The Creator, the One who walks with him and whose eyes brighten with love at each interaction, reassures him. The man falls asleep, a deep sleep of peace and trust, and awakens to find beside him a woman.

Her first sensation is of warm breath, God breathing life into her nostrils. Her eyes flutter open, her heart imprints with love for this creator God, who has poured life into her.

They are man and woman. She has yet to be named; she doesn't receive her name until they have roamed freely about the luscious garden and sampled the forbidden.

Only after the results of their disobedience become clear in the form of the cursing of the ground and the promise that they will not live forever but will taste death—only then is the woman given a name.

Adam calls her Eve, the "mother of all the living."

The woman, who tempted her husband and set death in motion, receives a name meaning "life" or "life producer." This is a stunning fidelity for Adam—a declaration of forgiveness and faith.

Her name holds the promise that though her choices resulted in death, spiritually and physically, for all of us, somehow, somewhere, down through the generations, life would return, the possibility of spiritual life. And though we each taste death as we return to the dust, we each, now, through the death and life of Christ Jesus, can experience life.

Though we make choices daily that are death-choices—clinging to anger, resentment, or lethargy and embracing selfishness, wrapping our arms around tangibles that money and work purchase—though we daily walk the line between life and death, whether man or woman, we have the potential to be life producers.

Whether we ever reproduce physically, we have the choice to reap life, to sow seeds bearing fruit for eternity. By investing in the lives of others and seeing each encounter as an opportunity to give life, we, too, become life producers.

My friend Gail is a soul-model for me and a life producer. She demonstrates in every encounter the life and love she received from a gracious and redeeming God. We met for dinner, and her blue eyes sparkled with interest and humor. When the waiter appeared, she turned to him with animation. "Is this a long-term career for you?" He opened the book of his life to her. He was an early-elementary teacher, this was a summer job, and he couldn't imagine doing anything other than teaching. When I commented to Gail later about her conversation starter, she said, "I try to develop a relationship with everyone I meet." Her interactions produce life.

Eve, though she set death in motion, was given the possibility of offering life. And we bear her trait—life giver—as we continue the legacy, as we find our life in Christ and lead others to that life.

LISTEN

"But thanks be to God, who always leads us as captives in Christ's triumphal procession and uses us to spread the aroma of the knowledge of him everywhere. For we are to God the pleasing aroma of Christ among those who are being saved and those who are perishing" (2 Cor. 2:14–15 NIV).

LEARN

"Each day of life we chisel our influence into the hearts and lives of others. Christ is the artist. You are his tool. Only you can decide how you will allow the Master Craftsman to use your life. 'One cannot transform a world except as individuals in the world are transformed, and individuals cannot be changed except as they are molded in the hands of the Master'" (Coleman and Farrel).

LIVE

When do you choose death instead of life? When do you choose life rather than death?

How do you feel and react when you hear yourself called "life producer"?

When do you see God producing life in you and through you in others?

37

FINDING LIFE BETWEEN TWO GARDENS

In spite of the name "life giver," death rippled quickly upon Eden's evacuation. Only when Eve's third child, Seth, had a son did people begin to once again call upon the name of the Lord. Like wayward seed from the cottonwood trees, the Israelites blew around on the winds of surrounding religions, practices, and morals (or lack thereof). Finally, after reaching the Promised Land for the second time and setting up the cities, their leader, Joshua, prepared to die. He called the people to take a stand: Would they serve the false gods of their imprisonment, or would they serve the God who delivered them from slavery into freedom? Joshua was stern with the Israelites and firm in his own choosing, and the Israelites responded with earnest humility.

So do we. And like Joshua's fickle kinfolk, we forget to serve God, forget that each choice brings either life or death. And in the stony, flowerless terrain between two gardens, we choose *self*, the old self, the self-focused self. Wallowing in this mud should convince us of life

choices. But we forget, again, when someone hurts or dis-
pleases us, life gets rocky, or fear digs its rake into our
turf. And we choose to serve ourselves, not God.

So it goes. A rigorous, exhausting, self-defeating
circling of good intentions vying with egocentric hearts,
like boxers in a ring.

Choosing life also means choosing death. This is a
paradox, choosing to die to temporary pleasures, to self-
indulgence at another's expense. But this is true in the
garden, every garden: "What you sow does not come to
life unless it dies. When you sow, you do not plant the
body that will be, but just a seed, perhaps of wheat or of
something else" (1 Cor. 15:36–37 NIV). We don't sow
oak trees; we drop acorns into the ground. The acorn
dies and then becomes a new life-form, a tree.

I dislike this truth, but it is so: We must die to ourselves in order to live a new life in Christ Jesus. And
daily we must choose life. Thankfully, though we so
often take the fruit into our own hands, demanding our
own way, we can also daily choose to move back into
the presence of Christ, the One who died, that we might
ever live. Through Christ's death, we find life.

LISTEN

"Joshua said to all the people, 'Thus says the LORD,
the God of Israel . . . "I gave you a land on which you
had not labored, and cities which you had not built, and

you have lived in them; you are eating of vineyards and olive groves which you did not plant." Now, therefore, fear the LORD and serve Him in sincerity and truth; and put away the gods which your fathers served beyond the River and in Egypt, and serve the LORD. If it is disagreeable in your sight to serve the LORD, choose for yourselves today whom you will serve. . . . As for me and my house, we will serve the LORD'" (Josh. 24:2, 13–15).

LEARN

Choose for yourself today: encouragement, not criticism; a smile, not a frown; forgiveness, not resentment; love, not hatred; praise, not pouting; relationship, not isolation; letting go of, not clinging to; grace, not grousing; growth, not stasis; dances, not dirges; feasts of spirit, not famine; beauty, not ugliness; servanthood, not self-focus; life, not death.

LIVE

What is a death choice you have made? How did you, or could you, turn it into a life choice?

When is it most difficult to choose life? Is there one area, one relationship, of primary struggle?

When have you experienced life-giving choices and the empowerment of Christ?

38

CHRIST IN THE GARDEN

In the garden of Eden, Adam's disobedience set death in motion. When Jesus chose obedience, He reversed the whole process. Christ's death set *life* in motion. His entire purpose was redemption: to fulfill that which began in Eden, to bring to an end the curses resulting from Adam and Eve's capitulation. His whole life propelled Him to the work done in Gethsemane, then to the hill shaped like a skull, and on into the garden in which was a new tomb, a now-empty tomb.

From the time Christ breathed His last breath and the earth quaked, the veil split in half and the earth gave up its dead, from then until we return to the tomb on resurrection Sunday, the first day of the week—indeed, the first day of new life—we have no record. The court reporters, paparazzi, and photojournalists were barred entrance from the final round when Christ wrestled with the serpent, when He fulfilled the promise in Genesis 3:15: "He shall bruise you on the head, and you shall bruise him on the heel."

Here's what we do know, however: With His momentous appearance following His death, Christ fulfilled the law, abolished the curse, and stands as the risen Lord, having canceled the death sentence, crushed the serpent, and become our light, bread, and rest. He has despised the shame of the cross and given us tools to stand against the disfigurement of shame. Jesus established for us the possibility of walking in unbroken fellowship with God. The Light of the World has withstood the darkness of temptation, treason, violence, and night. Jesus lived the life of an exile and died the death of a criminal and scapegoat, being crucified outside the gates. His entire life and even His death looked like a failure, yet it was in truth a resolution of all the curses and problems that had sprouted up since Eden.

And here's something else, one more amazing fulfillment, one more piece of evidence of God's provision for us from Eden to Gethsemane, and in this land between — when God created Adam and Eve, He breathed the breath of life into them. Outside of Eden, en route to the Promised Land, the breath of God dried up the Red Sea so the Israelites could cross on dry ground. And when Jesus hung on the cross, He "uttered a loud cry, and breathed His last. . . . When the centurion, who was standing right in front of Him, saw the way He breathed His last, he said, 'Truly this man was the Son of God!'" (Mark 15:37, 39). His very breath bore witness to His identity.

But the story doesn't stop there. When Christ appeared to the disciples after triumphing over the grave, He found them cowering in a closed room for "fear of the Jews." Twice He told them, "Peace be with you," and then, "'As the Father has sent Me, I also send you.' And when He had said this, *He breathed on them* and said to them, 'Receive the Holy Spirit'" (John 20:19–22, emphasis added). With that breath, Christ reestablished the permanent presence of God within the believer, enabling each of us to live fully in the garden of life.

Christ's work in the garden, His very breath, is an invitation to us to move out of the garden where life became death and into the garden where death became life.

LISTEN

"We were therefore buried with him through baptism into death in order that, just as Christ was raised from the dead through the glory of the Father, we too may live a new life" (Rom. 6:4 NIV).

LEARN

"So the cross not only brings Christ's life to an end, it ends also the first life, the old life, of every one of His true followers. It destroys the old pattern, the Adam pattern, in the believer's life, and brings it to an end. Then the God who raised Christ from the dead raises the believer and a new life begins" (Tozer, *Root*).

LIVE

Where do you need the life-giving breath of Christ right now?

How are you traversing the land between Eden and Gethsemane?

What do you see God doing during the journey?

39

FUTURE IN THE GARDEN

Crushing fatigue bowed my body. I propped myself on my elbow during a layover in Birmingham's airport. Like a horse sleeps standing up, my head bobbed over my work. I tried to write in my journal, but my eyelids slammed like trapdoors with broken springs. I refocused, then opened the Scriptures to Matthew 28:1–10, the story of Mary Magdalene and the other Mary.

As sunrise shattered the dark of night, the two Marys made their way to the garden tomb. They knew its location, because they sat watch over the tomb when Jesus was buried. They also knew a huge stone sealed the entrance. But an angel of the Lord had rolled away the stone and perched atop it. The guards shook with fear, becoming like dead men, the Scriptures say, because the angel's appearance was like lightning and his garment as white as snow. And to the women, the angel's first words were, "Do not be afraid" (28:5). Then the angel delivered the Lord's message to the women: "He is not here, for He has risen, just as He said. Come, see the place where He was lying. Go quickly and tell His disciples that He has risen from the dead; and behold, He is going ahead of you into Galilee, there you will see Him; behold, I have told you" (20:6–7). The two Marys ran "with fear and great joy" (28:8) into the future and into their calling.

I tensed with their conflicting emotions and felt the pulling and pounding of their hearts. Not much is known about the other Mary, but for Mary Magdalene, life had meant death until meeting Jesus; now His death threatened to undo everything. She lost her future standing at the cross and then watching at the tomb. With her Lord crucified and buried, she thought her life over and her future dead. But she ran in obedience into her calling: the first evangelist, the bearer of good news and ran straight into Jesus himself. And His words? "Do not be afraid" (28:10).

While we, too, lost our future in Eden, in the garden after Gethsemane we hear the first calling to go and tell the others (John 20:17). How do we respond, in light of our journey through the gardens of God?

Whatever the future holds, the Lord Jesus himself goes before us into it, even as He went before Mary. And if Christ is with us in the future, then truly we can hear and heed the angel's words and the words of Christ: "Do not be afraid." We can run with joy, even in the midst of fear.

I waited in that airport as a major project wrapped up. My future felt shaky; this project had been life-giving and financially supporting for nearly a year. Especially in weariness, despair leans close, and I confess to both a fear of that future and a dimming of joy.

A child's squeal jerked my heart to life. Every child's squeal becomes my own child's, and I leaned around a pillar to see a little boy, possibly two years old, with a shock of thick, black hair and lovely olive skin, move away from his mother, hands outstretched, reaching, eyes alight. His smile shot joy through me. He headed for something beyond my sight. The mother hesitated and started to pull him onto the moving walkway with her. Then she nodded, receiving some assurance from behind the pole. The child toddled ahead with glee.

I leaned farther around the column to put a visual with the audible joy. The toddler stood eye to eye with a calm, puppy-sized lab on a leash. The puppy pressed a wet muzzle to the entranced boy's nose, and tiny hands stroked the chocolate, velvet ears. They stood this way, puppy and boy, fast friends.

I thought I would pop with joy. Smiling an enormous smile, I glanced about to enjoy the moment with other observers. But cell phones, laptops, and file folders occupied the heads all around. They'd missed a moment in a million. So, nearly, had I, awash with fatigue.

I kept watch, then, and try to do so now, when fear of the future or preoccupation drains me. A joy watch. Keeping watch that day, tears nearly spurted when I saw the girl with the bulging backpack talking with animation to the parents flanking her sides. A dad carrying a baby. More joy pounded. A tall father exclaimed, picked up a preteen girl off the rolling sidewalk, hugged her, and pressed her to his chest. They strode off together, he altering his steps and his posture to bend near, to catch every nuance.

I felt as if the Holy Spirit came upon me, flooding me with a joy long dormant, like a tree in winter suddenly greeting the sun with billions of blossoms spilling from its fingertips.

For the final joy watch before I boarded the plane, a happy, high-pitched, girlish scream turned my head. Two flight attendants hurled themselves into each other's arms, laughing and crying. What a scene of friendship— exuberant, loud, unashamed, flushed of face, and smiling nonstop.

Perhaps, I thought, that was how Mary Magdalene wanted to greet her Lord and teacher.

LISTEN

"I have set the LORD continually before me; because He is at my right hand, I will not be shaken. Therefore my heart is glad and my glory rejoices; My flesh also will dwell securely. For You will not abandon my soul to Sheol; nor will You allow Your Holy One to undergo decay. You will make known to me the path of life; in Your presence is fullness of joy; in Your right hand there are pleasures forever" (Ps. 16:8–11).

"Now all these things are from God, who reconciled us to Himself through Christ and gave us the ministry of reconciliation, namely, that God was in Christ reconciling the world to Himself, not counting their trespasses against them, and He has committed to us the word of reconciliation. Therefore, we are ambassadors for Christ, as though God were making an appeal through us; we beg you on behalf of Christ, be reconciled to God. He made Him who knew no sin to be sin on our behalf, so that we might become the righteousness of God in Him" (2 Cor. 5:18–21).

LEARN

"Passion is the roller coaster ride that can happen when you follow Jesus Christ. It is the breathtaking, thrill-filled, bone-rattling ride of a lifetime where every moment matters and all you can do is hang on for [dear life]. When you become a Christian, when you decide to follow Christ, you decide in favor of passion. Jesus came to forgive us of our sin, yes, but His mission was also to introduce us to the passion of living. Most people believe that following Jesus is all about living *right*. *Not true*. Following Jesus is all about living *fully*" (Yaconelli).

LIVE

What fears of the future thump in your heart?

Where is Jesus in the midst of your fear? What does He say to you?

What longing do you experience in terms of your relationship with Christ?

40

A LIVING HOPE

In this garden, the garden of the new tomb, the garden where Christ has been raised from the dead, no cherubim with flaming sword waits to bar entrance as in Eden. In this garden, the angel meets us and says, "Do not be afraid" (Matt. 28:5). After the resurrection, every instance of Jesus' interactions with others was full of grace and peace. He said repeatedly, "Do not be afraid" and "Peace be with you" (see Matt. 28:10; John 20:19, 21, 26). The triumphant Christ demonstrates resurrection life: If He has conquered the last enemy, death, we truly have nothing to fear.

In Eden the Trinity created Adam and Eve joyfully, generously, and in God's own image. After their sin, Adam and Eve's children were born in their own image. And yet, the garden—of Eden and Gethsemane—is about life, about newness of life. Throughout the Scriptures, we hear God promising, "Behold, I will do something new, now it will spring forth; will you not be aware of it? I will even make a roadway in the wilderness, rivers in the desert" (Isa. 43:19). We hear Christ assuring us, "I am the resurrection and the life; he who believes in Me will live even if he dies" (John 11:25). "I will give you a new heart and put a new spirit within you" (Ezek. 36:26). "Old things passed away; behold, new things have come" (2 Cor. 5:17).

God doesn't sow death in this garden—except the death of that defaced image. In Christ, the last Adam, the very image of God, we are made new. All our lives are about being changed, transformed, morphed, into the image of Christ, our very nature and character morphing more and more into that of Christ. "For as in Adam all die, so also in Christ all will be made alive" (1 Cor. 15:22).

The image, rubbed out in Eden, is being restored daily as we move closer to the completion of Christ's work in Gethsemane. After traveling from Eden to Gethsemane, the truth breaks open tomb-cold hearts. The entire journey between these two gardens is about restoration, restoring us to the image of God, that we might again walk with God in newness of life. And we know now that everything we encounter en route to the garden—every rock, thistle, and snake—is a gardening tool to continue bringing forth in us the life of Christ. To love, touch, bless, heal, challenge, and call forth like Christ in this world.

What can we say to this? "Blessed be the God and Father of our Lord Jesus Christ, who according to His great mercy has caused us to be born again to a living hope through the resurrection of Jesus Christ from the dead" (1 Pet. 1:3). In this long exodus from Eden, where we lost our lives, we finally find our lives in Gethsemane.

Friend, what an amazing invitation, to come to the garden and walk with Jesus in newness of life. And in the final garden, when we walk together, we'll never tire of telling the story of Christ's life in us, with us, for us, and through us. From Eden to Gethsemane and all the way to heaven.

LISTEN

"The LORD will comfort Zion; He will comfort all her waste places. And her wilderness He will make like Eden, and her desert like the garden of the LORD. Joy and gladness will be found in her, thanksgiving and sound of a melody" (Isa. 51:3).

LEARN

Death cannot keep its prey,
Jesus my Savior,
He tore the bars away,
Jesus my Lord!
Up from the grave He arose;
With a mighty triumph o'er His foes;
He arose a victor from the dark domain,
And He lives forever, with His saints to reign.

He arose! He arose!
Hallelujah! Christ arose!
—Robert Lowry

"O Father of life, we praise thee that one day thou wilt take thy poor crooked creatures, and give them bodies like Christ's, perfect as his, and full of thy light. Help us to grow faster—as fast as thou canst help us grow. Help us to keep our eyes on the opening of thy hand, that we may know the manna when it comes. O Lord, we rejoice that we are thy making, though thy handiwork is not very clear in the outer man as yet. We bless thee that we feel thy hand making us. What if it be in pain! Evermore we hear the voice of the potter above the hum and grind of his wheel. Father, thou only knowest how we love thee. Fashion the clay to thy beautiful will. To the eyes of men we are vessels of dishonor, but we know thou dost not despise us, for thou hast made us, and thou dwellest with us. Thou hast made us love thee, and hope in thee, and in thy love we will be brave and endure. All in good time, O Lord. Amen" (MacDonald, *Paul*).

LIVE

Where do you need a sense of Christ's peaceful presence now?

Describe yourself made new in the image of Christ.

If you could sum up your journey in a paragraph titled "Finding My Life," how would it read? Is there someone with whom you could share that journey?

SMALL GROUP GUIDE

First, lay aside all worry that you won't have enough to talk about during this time together. Trust God; trust the Holy Spirit; trust that Christ has brought your group together for deep purposes. Don't be afraid of silence; most people are, but silence gives God space to speak and space for us to listen. Finally, don't try to fix the problems that arise in people's lives. Just be present to one another, love well, and judge not. Souls, like gardens, grow best with kindness.

GATHERING

As you gather, open with prayer. Consider beginning with a hymn or worship song for Lent.

GROUP DISCUSSION

Discussion can proceed informally. Whether you have an official leader or someone facilitates from the side, the features in this book lend themselves to the group process. You may want to allocate ten to twenty

minutes for this section, if you intend to work through
the book's elements during the group time.

Ask one another:

- What spoke to you?
- What did you underline or mark? Why?
- Where do you have questions?
- Where did God stir your heart, move you to tears,
  or challenge you?
- How do you see the elements of your life this past
  week aligning with the truth you're finding here?

APPLICATION

Listen

The Scriptures chosen correlate with the theme of
each chapter. Try reading the passage aloud as a group.
Or divide the group in half; one group reads the passage
to the other group. Then switch. Read it slowly and with
feeling, rather than robotically.

Or read Scripture using *lectio divina*, or sacred reading,
described in the introduction to this book. One person reads
the selection aloud, slowly, without undue inflection. The
group waits, listening for a phrase, word, or line that
quickens the individual's spirit. Wait with that soul response.

Then, turn to the person next to you, and whisper the
word or phrase that spoke to you. This isn't a paragraph or

a dissertation. Just softly repeat what you heard literally from the Word. Without hurrying, the leader reads the selection aloud again, twice more, with the same process.

Then ask God, "What would You want me to do with this?" Share what God seems to be prodding you to do, to apply, from the Scripture. This is strictly a time of applying the specific Scripture, not a time for explanation or chatter.

Pray for the person next to you for God's help in applying the Word.

Learn

Invite someone to read this quote aloud. Read it for content, for contrast, and to compare with the daily subject. What does it mean? How does it expand the day's meditation? How does it apply? Do you agree? Disagree? Why?

Live

These are questions that someone might ask who cares about our continued growth, healing, and developing — someone who wants to see us bloom on this journey. Designed to prod, poke, and root out issues and expose them to the sun and Son, these questions may evoke tenderness or possibly a reluctance to answer. Still, they are asked so that we can find our lives in Christ, so we can become who we are created to be.

Remember that we don't have to fix one another's problems, point out another's sin, or control someone's life. If you sense this happening, gently draw the group back to the question and to its application. We can't force growth; only God brings the growth. Don't worry about silence, and make every effort to honor another's pain or tears without fixing either or shaming another by your reaction.

Try to keep the conversation moving around the group, so that one person doesn't monopolize the discussion. It is unlikely that you will be able to answer all the questions during a one- or two-hour meeting.

PRAY

Close in prayer, so that God sandwiches the time together with the Holy Spirit's presence and power, compassion and conviction. For an alternate way to end, divide into pairs and pray for one another, then the leader closes the entire group in prayer.

For a free downloadable discussion guide that covers all forty readings in seven small-group sessions, visit wphresources.com/findinglife.

For more group ideas and resources, please visit www. JaneRubietta.com. If your group is interested in a video conference call with Jane Rubietta, during or toward the end of your study together, please contact her at Jane@JaneRubietta.com.

REFERENCES

à Kempis, Thomas. As quoted in David Nystrom. *The NIV Application Commentary: James*. Grand Rapids, Mich.: Zondervan, 1997. Print.

Adams, Patch. *Gesundheit!: Bringing Good Health to You, the Medical System, and Society through Physician Serivce, Complementary Therapies, Humor, and Joy*. Rochester, Vt.: Healing Arts Press, 1998. Print.

Allender, Dan. *The Wounded Heart: Hope for Adult Victims of Childhood Sexual Abuse*. Colorado Springs: NavPress, 1990. Print.

Anderson, Ray S. *The Gospel According to Judas: Is There a Limit to God's Forgiveness?* Colorado Springs: NavPress, 1991. Print.

Augustine. *Confessions*. Trans. Henry Chadwick. Oxford: Oxford University Press, 1991. Print.

Austin, Lynn. *Among the Gods*. Minneapolis: Bethany, 2006. Print.

--- *Faith of My Fathers*. Minneapolis: Bethany, 2006. Print.

Bonhoeffer, Dietrich. *The Cost of Discipleship*. New York: Touchstone, 1959. Print.

--- *Life Together: The Classic Exploration of Faith in Community*. New York: Harper & Row, 1954. Print.

--- *A Testament to Freedom: The Essential Writings on Dietrich Bonhoeffer*. Eds. Geffrey Kelly and Burton Nelson. New York: HarperCollins, 1995.

Brainard, Mary Gardner. As quoted in Calvin Miller. *The Unchained Soul: A Devotional Walk on the Journey into Christlikeness from the Great Christian Classics*. Minneapolis: Bethany House, 1998. Print.

Brother Andrew. *For the Love of My Brothers: Unforgettable Stories from God's Ambassador to the Suffering Church*. Minneapolis: Bethany House, 1998. Print.

Cameron, Julia. *The Artist's Way: A Spiritual Path to Higher Creativity*. New York: G. P. Putnam's Sons, 1992. Print.

Chesterton, G. K. *Chaucer*. Kansas City, Mo.: Sheed & Ward, 1956. Print. Chesterton Biography Series.

--- *Lunacy and Letters*. Kansas City, Mo.: Sheed & Ward, 1958. Print.

--- *Tremendous Trifles*. As quoted in George Marlin, Richard Rabatin, and John Swan, eds. *The Quotable Chesterton: A Topical Compilation of the Wit, Wisdom and Satire of G. K. Chesterton*. San Francisco: Ignatius Press, 1986. Print.

Coleman, Robert. As quoted in Pam Farrel. *Woman of Influence: Ten Traits of Those Who Want to Make a Difference*. Downers Grove, Ill.: InterVarsity Press, 1996. Print.

Condor, Bob. "Feeling Better Might Mean Seeing the Light." *Chicago Tribune* 25 June 2000, sec. 13. Print.

Dravecky, Jan. *A Joy I'd Never Known: One Woman's Triumph Over Panic Attacks and Depression*. Grand Rapids, Mich.: Zondervan, 1996. Print.

Edgar, Mary S. "God Who Touchest Earth with Beauty." *United Methodist Hymnal*. Nashville: Abingdon, 1964. Print.

Gabriel, Charles. "I Stand Amazed in the Presence." *Cyber Hymnal*. 1905. Web. 8 Oct. 2013. <http://cyberhymnal.org/htm/i/s/isaithep.htm>.

Hallowell, Edward. *Connect: 12 Vital Ties That Open Your Heart, Lengthen Your Life, and Deepen Your Soul*. New York: Pantheon Books, 1999. Print.

Hemfelt, Robert, Frank Minerth, and Paul Meier. *We Are Driven: The Compulsive Behaviors America Applauds*. Nashville: Thomas Nelson, 1991. Print.

Julian of Norwich. *Revelations of Divine Love*. London: Penguin, 1998. Print.

--- As quoted in Denise Nowakowski Baker. *Julian of Norwich's Showings: From Vision to Book*. Princeton, N. J.: Princeton University Press, 1994. Print.

Kelly, Geffrey. "Prayer and Action for Justice: Bonhoeffer's Spirituality." *The Cambridge Companion to Dietrich Bonhoeffer*. Ed. John W. de Gruchy. Cambridge, UK: Cambridge University Press, 1999. Print.

Kierkegaard, Søren. "Quotes." *Good Reads*. Web. 24 Oct. 2013. <http://www.goodreads.com/author/quotes/6172.S_ren_Kierkegaard>.

Lowry, Robert. "Up from the Grave He Arose." *Hymn Site*. Web. 8 Oct. 2013. <http://www.hymnsite.com/lyrics/umh322.sht>.

Luther, Martin. "A Mighty Fortress Is Our God." *Cyber Hymnal*. 1529. Web. 8 Oct. 2013. <http://cyberhymnal.org/htm/m/i/mightyfo.htm>.

MacDonald, George. *Lilith: A Romance*. Radford, Va.: Wilder Publications, 2008. Print.

--- *Paul Faber, Surgeon*. Philadelphia: J. B. Lippincott & Co., 1879. Print.

--- *Unspoken Sermons*. London: Longmans, Green, and Co., 1895. Print.

Mains, Karen. *Comforting One Another: In Life's Sorrows*. Nashville: Thomas Nelson, 1997. Print.

Martí, José. *The Quotations Page*. Web. 8 Oct. 2013. <http://www.quotationspage.com/quote/9768.html>.

Matheson, George. "O Love That Wilt Not Let Me Go." *Cyber Hymnal*. 1882. Web. 8 Oct. 2013. <http://cyberhymnal.org/htm/o/l/oltwnlmg.htm>.

Miles, C. Austin. "In the Garden." *Cyber Hymnal*. 1912. Web. 8 Oct. 2013. <http://cyberhymnal.org/htm/i/t/g/itgarden.htm>.

Mote, Edward. "My Hope Is Built." *Cyber Hymnal*. 1834. Web. 8 Oct. 2013. <http://cyberhymnal.org/htm/m/y/myhopeis.htm>.

Nelson, F. Burton. "The Life of Dietrich Bonhoeffer." *The Cambridge Companion to Dietrich Bonhoeffer*. Ed. John W. de Gruchy. Cambridge, UK: Cambridge University Press, 1999. Print.

Nouwen, Henri. As quoted in Stephen Kendrick. "In Touch With the Blessing: An Interview with Henri Nouwen." *The Christian Century* 10 (1993). Print.

Potter-Efron, Ronald and Patricia Potter-Efron. *Letting Go of Shame: Understanding How Shame Affects Your Life*. New York: HarperCollins, 1989. Print.

Powell, Father John. *Happiness Is an Inside Job*. Allen, Tex.: Tabor Publishing, 1989. Print.

Rhodes, Tricia McCary. *Contemplating the Cross: A 40 Day Pilgrimage of Prayer*. Minneapolis: Bethany, 1998. Print.

--- *Taking Up Your Cross: The Incredible Gain of the Crucified Life*. Minneapolis: Bethany, 2000. Print.

Ryrie, Charles C. *The Ryrie Study Bible*, Chicago: Moody Bible Institute, 1978. Print.

Schmemann, Alexander. *For the Life of the World: Sacraments and Orthodoxy*. Crestwood, N.Y.: St. Vladimir Seminary Press, 1973. Print.

Sheen, Fulton J. As quoted in Benedict J. Groeschel, ed. *The Journey Toward God*. Ann Arbor, Mich.: Servant Publications, 2000. Print.

Swenson, Richard. *Margin: Restoring Emotional, Physical, Financial, and Time Reserves to Overloaded Lives*. Colorado Springs: NavPress, 1992. Print.

Tan, Amy. *The Joy Luck Club*. New York: Putnam, 1989. Print.

Temple, William. *Christianity and Social Order*. U.K.: Shepheard-Walwyn, 1984. Print.

Thoene, Bodie. *In My Father's House*. Minneapolis: Bethany, 1992. Print. Shilo Legacy Series.

Tozer, A. W. *The Pursuit of God*. Harrisburg, Pa.: Christian Publications, Inc., n.d. Print.

--- *The Root of Righteousness*. Harrisburg, Pa.: Christian Publications, Inc., 1955. Print.

Umidi, Joseph L. *Confirming the Pastoral Call: A Guide to Matching Candidates and Congregations*. Grand Rapids, Mich.: Kregel, 2000. Print.

Watts, Isaac. "Joy to the World." *Cyber Hymnal*. 1719. Web. 8 Oct. 2013. <http://cyberhymnal.org/htm/j/o/joy world.htm>.

Webster, Douglas D. *SoulCraft: How God Shapes Us through Relationships*. Downers Grove, Ill.: InterVarsity Press, 1999. Print.

Wiersbe, Warren. *With the Word: A Devotional Commentary*. Nashville: Thomas Nelson, 1991. Print.

Willmer, Haddon. "Costly Discipleship." *The Cambridge Companion to Dietrich Bonhoeffer*. Ed. John W. de Gruchy. Cambridge, UK: Cambridge University Press, 1999. Print.

Yaconelli, Michael. *Dangerous Wonder: The Adventure of Childlike Faith*. Colorado Springs: NavPress, 1998. Print.

ABOUT THE AUTHOR

Jane Rubietta has a degree in marketing and management from Indiana University School of Business, and attended Trinity Divinity School in Deerfield, Illinois.

Jane's hundreds of articles about soul care and restoration have appeared in many periodicals, including *Today's Christian Woman*, *Virtue*, *Marriage Partnership*, *Just between Us*, *Conversations Journal*, *Decision*, *Christian Reader*, and *Christianity Today*. She is a regular contributor to *Indeed* and *Significant Living*. Some of her books include: *Quiet Places: A Woman's Guide to Personal Retreat*; *Come Along: A Journey to More Intimate Faith*; *Come Closer: A Call to Life, Love, and Breakfast on the Beach*; *Grace Points: Growth and Guidance in Times of Change*; *Resting Place: A Personal Guide to Spiritual Retreat*; and *How to Keep the Pastor You Love*.

She is a dynamic, dramatic, vulnerable, humorous speaker at conferences and retreats and pulpits around the world. Jane particularly loves offering respite and soul care to people in leadership as well as local churches. She has worked with Christian leaders and laity in Japan, Mexico, the Philippines, Guatemala, Europe, the US, and Canada.

Jane's husband, Rich, is a pastor, award-winning music producer, and itinerant worship leader. They have three children, and make their home surrounded by slightly overwhelming garden opportunities in the Midwest.

For more information about inviting Jane Rubietta to speak at your church, conference, retreat, or banquet, please contact her at:

Jane@JaneRubietta.com
www.JaneRubietta.com